Seeing God

HOPE FOR A NEW LAND

SHAWANDA R. RANDOLPH

Seeing God: Hope For A New Land
by Shawanda R. Randolph

No part of this book may be reproduced in any written, electronic, recording, or photocopying without written permission of the publisher or author.

Scripture quotations, unless otherwise annotated, are NRSV are taken from the New Revised Standard Version of the Bible, copyright 1989, by the Division of Christian Education of the National Council of the Churches of Christ in the United States of America. Used by permission.

Scripture quotations marked NIV are taken from **THE HOLY BIBLE, NEW INTERNATIONAL VERSION®, NIV® Copyright © 1973, 1978, 1984, 2011 by Biblica, Inc.® Used by permission. All rights reserved worldwide.**

Copyright © 2019 by Fresh Manna Ministries. All rights reserved.

Visit the author's Web site: Shawandarandolph.com

ISBN-13: 978-1-7332731-0-7

Deeper Cries

It is through the soul the heart cries out from the deep

Searching...longing for answers to what can make one whole and complete.

The answers to what you need have always been in front of you all along

It has been an outstretched hand, waiting to guide you to a place called home.

A place where you can find rest

A place where you can find peace

A place where there is beauty and full of happiness

A place where there is love

A place where there is joy

A place that does not discriminate if you are a girl or a boy

A place of hope

A place of no despair

A place where you can leave all of your cares

A place of patience

A place of light

A place that cares not if you are black or if you are white

Where is this place?

I was hoping you would ask

For imagining such a place in your mind seems quite a heavy task

I promise you, such a place does exist

If you would only open your eyes to see

For the place of home is closer than you would believe

For many would think this is a far-off land,

But this place of grace is right in the Father's Hands

If only we would take off the blinders of our personal views

Which can sometimes become a hindrance to ourselves, and leave us confused,

We can begin to REFOCUS moving in a new direction, toward that marvelous light

Walking towards the beautiful eyes that SEE us daily and the loving outstretched hands ready to give us a new outlook on LIFE.

Table of Contents

Introduction: Seeking New Vision - Removing Blinders............vii

Part I: FINDING HOPE WITH GOD... 1

    Hope For Change 3

    Removing Barriers 19

    Removing Boundaries and Limitations.............................35

    The Light of Grace...69

    Starting Over..77

Part II: FINDING FAITH IN GOD 83

    Faith To See 85

    Faith To Overcome...89

    Faith to Trust..93

    Faith To Believe 103

Part III: THE LEADERSHIP PERSPECTIVE 115

    The Power of Influence 117

    The Honor Code 129

    How Are You Leading? 143

Part IV: A NEW LIFE OF FREEDOM WITH GOD 153

    References...193

INTRODUCTION

Seeking New Vision - Removing Blinders

I recall, early at a young person, the sincere desire of wanting to know God. In my innocence, I knew He was a loving God even though I saw so much around me that presented mixed representations of love and suffering. I have early childhood memories of exposure to death and seeing people grieve over the loss of loved ones can be detrimental to a child, especially one that desired to know God, but somehow, death and grief were explained in a way that did not make me focus on the pain and suffering. This explanation helped me to not turn away from the desire of wanting to know God more.

Unfortunately, as I would continue to grow, stepping out further on my own and encountering more people, these "experiences" of how God was portrayed would vary. The encounters would have a profound effect on how I would see God, for myself. They would also affect how I felt about my relationship with God.

I would hear religious people speak of the rules and regulations you must follow, like a formula or checklist that would guarantee you a place in God's Kingdom. I would study the church doctrine (or guidelines) making notes in the book, with questions about things that did not seem to make sense. I questioned these rules, as they appeared obscure and distorted God's image. Many of these rules, I would openly question. These questions were often met with disconcertment or defensiveness.

INTRODUCTION

I recall a significant youth gathering where I respectfully questioned many of the practices we were charged with upholding. I wondered why no one else questioned these rules. Instead, they just sat accepting without explanation. Unlike a disrespectful or blatantly rebellious child, I questioned for understanding, as I did not understand where God referenced these specific practices in the Bible. Furthermore, the explanation from the teacher was quite unsatisfactory. She related everything to living Holy, being saved, and allowing us to live either in Heaven or hell.

We were taught that simple things like playing with dice or cards were a damnation, therefore would have a profound effect on our relationship with God. Furthermore, we could be condemned to a life in hell because such things were unholy. This applied to all music that was not gospel or "Christian," and even our clothing, where women were only allowed to wear skirts and dresses. And not all were acceptable, as dresses and skirts must be a certain length, or you would receive the all disapproving look. The wearing of pants implied we were dressing like a man, and scripture was used to back up the issue of clothing. Honestly, everything seemed off to me. How did they come up with this interpretation, I wondered? So, I posed questions.

"Why are you equating dice to evil? My family spends time together playing Monopoly. It has dice, but the game is far from evil. The dice are used to move you around the board." These were my arguments to "push back" regarding one of the "can't do's" to "live Holy" and "please God." I was met with a befuddled look, coupled with a lengthy pause. I assumed she was unsure how to respond. The response I received was along the lines of, "but people use dice for gambling." I politely countered with, "but we are not gambling, so why are we

INTRODUCTION

banning dice? The same applies to cards. We play UNO. It's innocent. What is the issue?"

I never received a straight answer to my questions that day. Initially, I was met with more questions about the nature of the games we played. I remember throwing in other family games that used dice. I explained that some games helped with counting money, talking about property, and just overall innocent fun. The person thought maybe it was ok. She mentioned that if we were not gambling, it should be ok. I asked then why teach that dice are bad? Why say they are forbidden if it is really about how someone uses something? Needless to say, this became a frustrating encounter for both her and me. She would eventually move on, dismissing my questions. The same happened when I questioned the teachings of condemning everyone, that was not in the church, to hell or the condemnation of our clothing that was a barrier in our relationship with Christ. It was an interesting afternoon, and my questions were put off by a confused teacher. Why? I would argue that it is because something was traditionally taught without any real understanding as to why. Therefore, people believed what was bad because that is what they were told to think, and that is all they could see.

I saw something terribly wrong, not just about cards, dice, and clothing, but a bigger issue. The stumbling block of leading people to a healthy relationship with Christ. This burned in my heart and vexed me more than I understood. A fire was lit in me that would lead me to not just accept without being taught. I would be guided by those who had knowledge and understanding. Furthermore, I knew that someday, I wanted to be a part of something that would help people SEE truth, to SEE GOD CLEARLY.

INTRODUCTION

In *Seeing God, Hope For A New Land*, I take the time to address major issues that affect how we SEE, FEEL about, and RELATE to God. I examine the effects of practicing religious dogma without the understanding of its traditional roots. The purpose is to gain further insight into some long-standing practices we have essentially personalized, to realign them back to their original Biblical design. In doing so, we can remove obscurity and barriers to help people SEE the TRUE nature of YHWH...BELIEVING, once again, that He is God in Heaven and earth.

It is not God's desire to have lost generations. It was never a desire to have his people not know Him, mainly because their "ancestors" failed to properly teach them about Him. Too often, I have heard about how "this generation will be lost" or "...will need help." The truth is, the generations before believed that force-feeding something that some of them either did not embrace or did not understand was the best "nutrition" for the upcoming generation. It is not! Unfortunately, such practices are counterproductive. They exacerbate the issues by creating people that have more questions about how could a god that one claims to be so loving and kind, be so cruel or absent. It leaves, people with more unanswered questions about God and wondering where to find them while working to make their way in this world. The issue is not whether they are lost, but what barriers have been placed before them, hindering or preventing their relationship with Elohim, God the Creator.

Many rightfully refuse to accept everyone's belief without understanding. Can you blame them? Look at what we have made God appear to be in their eyes. It is time to see God clearly and change this distorted image of Him and how He works in our lives.

INTRODUCTION

It is time to feel that we can live freely with God by breaking down these atrocious human-made barriers. It is time to build more meaningful relationships with GOD and live a life more fulfilled!

Part I

FINDING HOPE WITH GOD

Hope For Change

How can we accomplish anything if we are constantly divided with one side fighting the other? Have we not had enough of one side exalting themselves over another? When will we ever learn?

Who is right? Who is wrong?

In a place where Christ was bringing us together, we have done everything we can to keep the division lines real.

It's your fault, no, it is hers. It's his fault, not it's theirs.

I would argue that everyone is to blame for calling out the other's name. There is no accountability or taking responsibility for personal actions.

God said, is it not good for Man to be alone. He created a helpmeet for Man. Together, they were given dominion over all things, caring for God's creation. Even in sin, they were still together. One blamed the other, but even then, God showed they were in this together as that is how He sent them out, having to be and work together, and maintaining their combined responsibilities. They would populate the earth together.

Now, we are separating more and more. I sometimes wonder if we thought how our actions and thoughts could lead us back to where we started, alone, isolated, eventually back in a dark place where no life existed. Extinct. Ashes to Ashes. Dust to Dust. Then I get this glimpse of hope.

My son recently asked what I wanted for Christmas. I could not think of anything I wanted him to give me that I did not already have from him. He's grown into a fine young man, pursuing his dreams despite obstacles he encounters. He tries to remain positive and make the most of life even when it seems the odds are stacked against him. What he has already given me is the gift that he continues to embrace for himself, HOPE. Hope for a better life. Hope for the future. Hope for a better tomorrow.

In a time where people are continuously at each other's throat spreading lines of division, I watch young people like my son working in the hope that the world we have created for them to live, will soon become a better place for their children to thrive. Reflecting over the past few years, I look at how we have grown and not all for the better.

We are reactive people than proactive people, and in too many ways, our reactions have caused us to live in increased fear and disarray. In turn, we have allowed these things to spill over into the lives of our children. Raising them to believe they must live in bubbles, isolation, division, and solitude, rather than embracing community.

We have raised our children to fear rather than have faith in community and allowing a community to help our children thrive. We have raised children to depend on their parents, making parents their gods. They cannot do anything or be anything without their parents and rely on solely the protection of their parents. Then we wonder why a generation appears to rise in rebellion. Their spirit is trapped and stifled by the oppressive authority of their parents' fear rather than faith.

Let's take a stroll down memory lane, thinking back to 9/11. Think of how the attack on this country instilled fear in the lives of people and how we reacted. While for a time, people began flocking together in solidarity and community, how long did that last? And were we really acting in solidarity or was it selective solidarity and community? After all, how many people began turning on our Muslim brothers and sisters? The discrimination against people increased tremendously and has not truly deceased. I call that living in fear and not faith.

As we began to travel security increased in our airports and let's be honest, have the acts of removing our shoes and checking the number of toiletries we carry onboard really made us safer? How many reports have we witnessed in the news, after that, of people still getting through with weapons since heightened security measures? Or does the illusion of the long wait times and all the people standing around with TSA apparel just make you feel better as you gripe about having to arrive at the airport 2-3 hours before your flight, only to run to the gate because you are still running behind to enjoy a "vacation?"

Ah, but can opt out to pay for a prescreen to verify you are potentially safe, therefore having less to take the same measure of others when passing through security.

Again, I pose the question, what illusion is this, and who is this really for to ease fear? What are we doing people? What environments are we raising our children in?

A few years ago, I sat in a church during a Bible study and unsure how or why the discussion led to homosexuality and the debate of gender-neutral bathrooms. I believe it was a "hot topic" during that time in the public, yet I must say I was so disgusted that I left, went home and prayed while weeping at the words I heard from members of the congregation and leaders. I could not believe that this place, where anyone should come to feel safe, the body of Christ was ignorantly discussing "outsiders: in such a negative fashion adding to the disturbing stereotypes that increases fear and hate rather than Faith and Hope.

What's interesting is how often you hear how the church must be different from the world. I suppose no one thinks about how the challenge also exists in how we live in Fear and Hate vs. Faith and Hope.

If the lines of division are drawn outside of the church as well as inside of the church, then where shall we find the light? Where shall we find Hope?

Still, today, looking around, these separatist lines are growing generations who "govern" while the generation "rising" are struggling to bring about change for they care not to live in the mess we have created. Unfortunately, it is an uphill battle, but I have faith that they will achieve something that we could not...Real Change!!

They should not and must not go at this alone. So, my gift I prayed for ...the miracle I prayed for is Change. A change in the mindset of people. A change in the heart of people. Why? Because our children want, desire, and deserve more than we have given them over the years. Why must they struggle to create change? Why must they fight against the barriers we have created, due to our fears which hinder their ability to thrive? Why are we not doing more to show them the value of community, rather than allowing them to fear everything and grow in isolation with limited ability to communicate?

Why make them dependent rather than independent, teaching them that safe does not mean "achieving everything" because failure and mistakes are lessons, we can learn from, making us resilient and better thinkers? Let's give them HOPE by starting to embrace differences among people, to give them something to look forward to, helping them to see and believe they are not in this fight alone. You know, we could learn a lot from our children if we open our hearts and minds.

Children start off innocent, full of love, and joy. They learn fears from us. We pass on what we are fearful of rather than teaching healthy boundaries. We instill our fears, biases, and beliefs, and unfortunately, not all beliefs are enhancements to our well-being. Perhaps, a revolution is necessary. Look at your children or those you influence. What are you teaching them? What tools are you providing to help them with life choices? How do you encourage Faith, Hope, Joy, Love, Trust, Peace, Community, and Communication? How often do you encourage them to step out and strive for something they desire, even if it is something you would never do? Or, do you spend time recreating them in your image rather than the image they were created to be, which leads to stifling their spirit and ability to fully thrive in their God Given Life?

When I was in the 10th grade about 15 years old. I shared with someone how I hated the idea that when people go through situations, everyone wants to tell them how to live or how they will forever live their life. In my case, I was told that as a survivor of abuse, my life was already predestined to turn out a certain way based on statistics. The statistics were I guess the norm. I wasn't buying it. I wanted my life to be a demonstration that this did not have to be the case. That just because a young woman was abused in any form, physically, mentally, or sexually, this would not define nor determine the rest of their life. People around them had no right to guide them in such a path.

I had no idea, then that I was in agreement with God's Word, and he would show me how. Over the years, he would open my eyes to see the life of those before me, demonstrating what I needed to help me reach my destiny. These individuals would not only show this physically but continuously share what was necessary through guidance and wisdom as well.

I have heard the saying, "People come in your life for a reason, a season, or a lifetime, you just need to determine which they fell into." I believe there is more to this. I believe that even if a person is in your life for a season or a lifetime, they are there for a reason. Too often, people overlook the importance of why they were connected. They fail to make the connection to their connections. You can learn something even from those you least expect. Think for a moment about the most common thing people do at the end of a year...begin disconnecting from people. The revelation of "I need to cut off negative people," or "everyone cannot go where I'm going," *suddenly* hits *every year* in December as one prepares for the new year.

It is a vicious cycle...

Would we need to keep repeating a cycle if we learned our lesson to start with? Before "suddenly" disconnecting, the real reflection should be, why were we connected in the first place? What was I supposed to learn from all of this? Surely, it may not be as simple as cutting off negative people. Perhaps the lesson is discovering why we make the decision to surround ourselves with the same types of people. Maybe, we have more in common with them than we realize and have not worked through this issue yet. Perhaps one has not learned the impact of our attitude in life and the results thereof. For everyone, the lessons are different.

Through connections, one can learn how to live as well as how not to live. The best example of this is that of a parent-child relationship. There are many others to utilize, but this always hits home for people. When you were younger, your parents (or a parental figure) would give you guidance and advice. Your younger self, knowing everything and nothing at the same time, felt you didn't need to listen to that advice. Later you would find that you eventually did some of the same things your parents did. Rather than learning the lesson verbally, you ended up learning the lesson through your own personal experience. Now, many would say, well we had to learn for ourselves, but I will push back to say, did you really? Perhaps, someone went before you, struggled and learned the hard way so that you would not have to. Perhaps, in what they went through, they were to become your guide, the one who would talk with you and warn you to say, HEY WATCH FOR THAT STUMBLING BLOCK. Perhaps, they were to help prevent you from falling as you learned from their experience. Perhaps, that pain was unnecessary for you, but you decided to unnecessarily experience it.

When you fell, that parent just helped you up and helped you move forward. If you really learned your lesson, you would normally turn and say, I'm sorry I should have listened. This is followed by a comforting parents voice, "it's ok...don't do it again."

Fast forward to life as we now know it. We still have these same figures or connections in our life that we learn from. Some are up close and personal, and some may be more distant but if we watch and listen closely we can learn a few things. These connections could be friends, family members, leaders, celebrities, business owners...anyone, even someone younger than you. Basically, anyone that has done something we have yet to experience, enter into, etc. Anyone that will guide us down the path we will soon travel.

Here is a basic example:

If you're destined to own a business you may unexpectedly find yourself around prominent and not so prominent entrepreneurs. It's common that people gravitate to the successful ones, but I challenge you to learn from those who were not as successful too. While it is great to learn what someone did to succeed it is just as important to learn why someone has struggled. Perhaps you would learn what to watch for, what to attempt to avoid...you would be prepared to see the stumbling block before you tripped and fell. Again, you can apply this to any area, you just have to begin to use a little wisdom in understanding the purpose of your connections. There is always a reason for your connections even if they are in your life for a short season or a lifetime.

Have you taken the time to examine your connections and why they exist? Are you making the most of your connections or are you undervaluing them? Don't waste time in your life by not learning from your connections and experiencing unnecessary situations.

As a young girl, I loved sitting, watching, and listening to my uncles. The thought of those memories overwhelms my heart. As an adult anytime my uncles are together, I feel like a little girl completely overjoyed and the truth is, I don't think they truly understand this.

See, my memories are of them standing together at church or in the home of my grandmother, together singing harmoniously. It's not about the music in the background, it's the music as they lift their voices to make a joyful noise unto The Lord in worship. My soul still gets full today as I am brought to tears whenever they get together and lift their voices in song to God. I learned to love to lift my voice in song to sing His praises and to worship Him, though not quite as beautiful as my uncles sound when they are together.

While some would rather run outside and play, nothing was more intriguing than sitting nearby listening to the uncles study, well actually, debate about the meaning of scriptures. I tell you, this would get interesting, but I thought these were some really smart guys. I admit it was also quite amusing to hear them challenge one another or disagree and I would chuckle. Nonetheless, I could not pull away until I heard whatever the final answer would be. Sometimes, they would be there a long time, longer than I could stay present but these discussions made me hungry beyond the basic things I heard when I rarely attended services. I wanted more, I wanted to learn more. These discussions made me read, research, and seek more in the Word of God. Always wanting more because of the example my uncles set and I found myself in seminary years later. A goal or dream I wanted to accomplish since I was a young person.

I learned there is always more. I learned to go deeper in and with God. Collective lessons are great, but so are the individual lessons and impartations from each of them. Rather than thinking about how my birth father was not present in my life or the pros and cons of having a step-father, I have come to realize that my Father in Heaven, God, provided me with more father figures than I could hope for and they would teach me invaluable life lessons.

My mother's six brothers have provided lessons of *Joy, Trust, Faith, Hope, Love, and Courage (strength)* that would not just help me as a woman but in my relationship with God. Now, that is powerful! With each uncle, they came along to provide the lesson I needed, and when I needed it the most. I would continue to draw on those lessons throughout my life. One would come through one uncle that I tend to borrow from his children because he has been like a father to me, his name is Michael Randolph. Now, uncle Mike, I believe has indeed been like a "Mordecai" in my life, helping to raise me and leading me to the plans God has for me. No matter what the situation is or has been, I can pick up the phone and call him. I have called to laugh, cry, tell my fears to, ask for help (in many ways), and no matter what he is always there.

When I am stuck and need to figure out what to do or how things are going to work, he is always reminding me of God's Word. He has been a teacher, sharing the word of God, teaching me exactly what I need to move me forward on my path. I love how I do even have to say much. When I call all I have to say is one thing and he just goes right for what I need. He hears what God is saying, gives it to me, and pushes me out a little further.

Whenever we speak, I always feel encouraged, empowered, and ready to take on whatever I need to. He truly pours into not only my dreams and goals but those of my son as well. To sweeten the deal, when there are times that I need a sweeter voice and another heart to hear from, I can call his wife, my aunt Laverne who for most of my childhood I had no idea this woman's first name was Sylvia, but that another story.

Anyway, this beautiful couple, whether they realize what they were doing over the years or not, have always given me and shown me hope. They would help the young woman who one day said she would change the world by helping people like herself realize life could be better than what "others" say, to do precisely that. They would help her...me realize, along this tough journey that started with personal healing, that anything is possible and no matter what, to just keep pushing forward. They would continue to give me hope for my future to give hope to others.

After years and years of study, research, meetings, volunteering, working, careers, and various aspects of ministry, with the guidance and direction of God, I started DeeCilla Comfort Center.

This faith-based nonprofit will help survivors of domestic violence, sexual assault, and trafficking. We plan on opening a campus with a transitional home for survivors ages 18-28. Residents will reside with DeeCilla Comfort Center for 12 months then move to independent living coupled with six months of transitional care and assistance. In his home we want to restore HOPE for the future to women survivors.

As a woman who first-hand understands the healing process it takes for a young adult that age, I want to give what was given to me...HOPE. Hope to understand that whatever dreams one had can become a reality and no matter what happened to you and help realize this is not who you are. This is not a label you must allow others to trap you behind or place you in a box, therefore defining who you or your life.

So, just as Michael and Sylvia Randolph would follow God and not only show me hope for my future but protect the hope God had shown me at 15. Just as they would guard my hope and be those safe keepers of my future so that no matter what my present situation appeared to be, I would continue to press forward. In the Michael and Sylvia House of Hope I will be a blessing to others and do the same, helping young people who believe there is no hope, realize hope still exists for them to have the life they always dreamed of. In turn, they will be equipped and empowered to do the same.

Part of the process of gaining what I would need to help others was understanding how I saw the world around me and what I would need to change. Before God would allow me to step forward, claiming to help make a difference in the life of someone else, He would ensure my journey or preparation would consist of teaching me to see as He does. I would need new sight and insight to aid in helping me to break barriers rather than being one in the lives of those he would connect with me.

"A call" comes with a path of preparation. Many times, we may attribute our years of education or studies as the path of preparation. I would attest that sometimes the path God places us on is also a guided journey from knowledge to understanding, that results in the most significant area of development. This way of preparation and development rightfully changes our perspectives, so our eyes become open to the world God has called us. Our views and understanding must change to align ourselves to live to work with Christ and make the greatest impacts.

Emmanuel Lartey implies the pitfalls, ministers may find themselves in, as they practice theology in a vacuum based on inherent assumptions, that all persons everywhere shared the same assumptions and presuppositions.[1] The challenge with this practice is it hinders our ability to connect or appropriately decipher the need for individuals, especially across cultures. He claims that "a person who only knows one culture, actually knows no culture."[2] It is amazing how God could change your perspective and understanding of culture, as he relates it to your "new" context. I would normally stand

---

[1] Emmanuel Y. Lartey, *Pastoral Theology in an Intercultural World* (Eugene: WIPF & STOCK, 2006), 45

[2] Lartey, *Pastoral Theology*, 49

proud knowing I was fortunate enough to be raised in culturally diverse areas. I know people from around the globe with many different ethnic backgrounds and have gained much understanding of their cultures. What God would reveal was how little I understood in the world of westernized "church culture" or culture of religion/faith, mainly outside of my own.

As God would call me to ministry, he further required a period of deeper discipleship, to grasp what it meant to surrender and follow as God would lead. This period of discipleship also enacted as a symbolic journey on "The Road to Damascus," following a conversion similar to apostle Paul. Taken on a journey through seminary, not merely to gain knowledge, yet to understand what this "call" would mean. A journey where my perspective not only about myself, but others, and perhaps the world they lived and how they met God, would evolve.

This would be imperative for the near future, as I would be "sent" to impact the lives of the unchurched and churched from various backgrounds. Like Paul, my ideas, and what I had been taught to believe and practice would become challenged. My vision would have to gain greater depth to see beyond the realms of my "learned norms." Instead, I would need to embrace how and why others may or may not have encountered Christ.

DeGroat speaks of St John's time in prison. This period of darkness, God seemed to use to prepare and refocus him to lead a movement he was called to.[3] As DeGroat describes the use positive use of darkness such as helping to cure our arro-

---

3 Chuck DeGroat, *toughest people to love: how to understand, lead, and love the difficult people in your life – including yourself* (Grand Rapids: William B. Eerdmans Publishing Company, 2014), 111

gance, blindness, and vacuum of empathy,[4] I am reminded of how Christ blinded Paul, only to have his eyes "reopened."[5] This was a time of revelation in which his entire way of seeing changed, as he now seemed to "see" through the lens of Christ. He now began to align himself with a new way of thinking and approaching others. Interestingly, we see different partnerships evolve, as well, with those he once "persecuted" though they may not have always agreed.

Often we are accustomed to seeing from our point of view, based on our life. This poses numerous challenges, especially when we must practice pastoral care beyond the context in which we may have been accustomed. Our minds must become open to looking beyond our assumptions and presuppositions so that we do not impose a set of beliefs,[6] rather we become capable of valuing the difference in cultures and placing theories alongside practice to facilitate necessary development.[7] To help with this facilitation, Lartey stresses the importance of collaboration and teamwork.[8] He implies the importance of communication and collaboration for effective ministry, especially the freedom to raise questions about each other's views.[9] In these collaborations, we eliminate the dangers of not meeting people in culture and context, thereby properly influencing healing and change. Such a collaboration was demonstrated at "the Council at Jerusalem" in Acts 15.

---

4 DeGroat, *toughest people to love*, 112
5 Acts 17, Bible, New Revised Standard Version (New York: Oxford University Press, 1989)
6 Lartey, *Pastoral Theology*, 45
7 Lartey, *Pastoral Theology*, 46
8 Lartey, *Pastoral Theology*, 86
9 Lartey, *Pastoral Theology*, 83

As God would launch me into a ministry in missionary work, the understanding of this journey becomes prevalent. Understanding, I would be taken out of the walls of what I learned as typical church, I further understood that my new context is a culture I was not initially considering. Thus, the reason to gain a new understanding of how others encounter Christ, as well as, have a diverse faith/belief community as members of my ministry team.

Larry Crab implies churches should become communities assuming the role in healing the wounded.[10]

---

10 Stephen Seamands, *Ministry in the Image of God: Trinitarian Shape of Christian Service* (Downers Grove: InterVarsity Press, 2005), 32

Removing Barriers

It is always painful to witness or hear separatist language, especially in the church. The lines of division using the grounds of living Holy, being Saved, or being the light as a means to essentially persecute individuals or groups of people who are supposedly different. I find it interesting that people who claim to worship or follow Christ fail to look at the historical background of the persecuted church and work to not become the new persecutors.

In the first three centuries, the historical church struggled in the stability of its relationship with the state, the Roman Empire. It would experience a long period of sporadic localized persecutions throughout Rome and Asia Minor,[11] which would hit its darkest era around 250 AD. During the 250 years of intermittent persecutions,[12] only a dozen of the fifty-four emperors went out of their way to persecute Christians with their decrees primarily against church property, the Scriptures, or clergy.[13]

Historical records and customs would paint a revealing tell, contrary to many misconceptions surrounding the details of

---

11 Justo Gonzalez, *The Story of Christianity* (New York: Harper-Collins, 2010), 47

12 Herbert B. Workman, *Persecution in the Early Church,* (1906), 106

13 www.religionfacts.com/persecution-early-church.

these persecutions. While there are few exceptions, notable persecutions were founded on misguided ideas surrounding teachings and practices of Christianity. These ideas, from the standpoint of the emperor, were a threat to the empire he must protect. This tension would create the greatest challenge in the church-state relationship, between the church and the empire, resulting in sporadic yet progressive persecutions. Persecutions that would eventually take a turn for the worse before the church received a final reprieve and finally became tolerated by the state, changing the trajectory of the church-state relationship for years to come. In the waking of a new era, the church-state relationship would have profound impacts upon the church, emperor, and the empire.

Sunset – Start of Persecutions

The most notorious acts of persecutions arguably noted came at the start and end of the church's persecution, under the reigns of Nero, 64 AD, and Diocletian, 303 AD. Around 64 AD, under Emperor Nero, persecutions were noted as uniformly severe, throughout the empire, compared to the remaining first and second centuries.[14] Not motivated by keeping justice in the empire, Nero used the torment and death of Christians for his and the people's amusement.[15] Not until the second century would we have more detailed accounts of Christian persecutions[16] told through the recorded life and death of martyrs. Historical letters would provide the tension between the church and state as emperors charged Christians with disloyalty to the empire or obstructing social order.

---

14 Gonzalez, *The Story of Christianity*, 47
15 Gonzalez, *The Story of Christianity*, 45
16 Gonzalez, *The Story of Christianity*, 49

Though Christianity was not outlawed, since the time of Emperor Trajan, the church would face still face accusations and forced to live in a constant state of uncertainty[17] due to misunderstandings surrounding their practice and teachings.[18] Expected to worship "the gods" as a demonstration of loyalty and acknowledgment of the emperor's right to rule,[19] when in violation, they were brought to trial and put to death for not abandoning their faith. Further accusations would include orgiastic celebrations,[20] cannibalism,[21] and participation in black magic.[22] Thus, the church and their implied rituals which did not align with roman purification rites and ceremonies were a threat to the emperor and the societal structure.[23] These series of conflicts would continue well into the third century. The dynamics would change for a time in the third century, as again the church is deemed a threat to Roman Order, but becomes persecuted empire-wide for eleven years.[24]

As the Roman Empire borders on the brink of economic demise, the church would face persecution on a greater scale. In 249 AD, Decius issues an edict for all inhabitants of Rome to sacrifice to the gods, which would also institute the first roman-wide persecution against Christians.[25] The intent was

---

17 Workman, *Persecution in the Early Church*, 201

18 Gonzalez, *The Story of Christianity*, 59

19 Gonzalez, *The Story of Christianity*, 50

20 Gonzalez, *The Story of Christianity*, 59

21 Gonzalez, *The Story of Christianity*, 60

22 Workman, *Persecution in the Early Church*, 130

23 William Klingshirn and Linda Safran, *The Early Christian Book (CUA Studies in Early Christianity)* (Washington, D.C.: Catholic University of America Press, 2007), 160

24 https://www.earlychurch.org.uk/persecution.php

25 J.B. Rives, "The Decree of Decius and the Religion of Empire," *The Journal of Roman Studies*, 1999, 1

not to target or single out Christians, they, however, had become a significant portion of the population,[26] despite the previous years of persecution. The edict was the emperor's response to please "the gods" responsible for giving Rome power and the empire prosperity, as the current state of the empire signified the gods were neglected and angry.[27] Unlike the Jews, Christians were not recognized as an independent religious entity, thus refusing to worship the gods for the sake of the empire was considered an act of treason. By sheer numbers, due to the spread of Christianity, the church was deemed the larger threat.

Saint Eusebius of Caesarea, historian of Christianity, would account a different motive. Saint Eusebius writes, "Decius, because of his hatred for Philip, stirred up a persecution against the churches, during which, when Fabian was perfected by martyrdom at Rome, Cornelius succeeded to the episcopacy."[28] Decius succeeded Philip and there are arguments questioning if Philip was a Christian, thus perhaps affecting the relationship between the church and state.[29] Eusebius implies that Philip had a friendly disposition toward the church, going beyond toleration though he never made Christianity legal.[30] The church would not receive the victory of official toleration from the state until 313 AD, but not before experiencing the

---

26 George Thomas Osborn, "Why Did Decius and Valerian Proscribe Christianity?" *Church History*, 1933, 67

27 Osborn, "Why Did Decius and Valerian Proscribe Christianity?" 67

28 Eusebius and Roy J. Defarrari, *Ecclesiastical History: The Fathers of the Church, (books 6-10)*, (Washington, DC: Catholic University of America Press, 2005), 65

29 Hans A. Pohlsander, "Philip the Arab and Christianity," *Historia Zaitschrift Fur Alte Geschichte*, 1980, 463

30 Pohlsander, "Philip the Arab and Christianity," 468

worst persecution in centuries since Nero.

The Darkest Night – The Worst of the Persecutions

What would eventually become known as the "Great" Persecution (303 – 311), would cause the greatest detriment to the church, before the church's ultimate liberation. In centuries past, the church expanded as news of martyrdom spread throughout the empire. The events surrounding the "Great" Persecution would have a contrary effect, as leaders would apostate to avert torture and death. Therefore, Diocletian's plan thought mostly instigated and influenced by Galerius,[31] to dismantle the church, responsible for Rome's instability and economic decline, would go un-faltered. Diocletian desired to return Rome to the more traditional gods, therefore restoring the *"pax deorum,"* "peace of the gods,"[32] initially influenced by meetings held with Galerius over the Christians refusal to support the military.[33]

Lactantius, supported the idea that Diocletian succumbed to powers of influence in promulgating edicts against Christians writing:

> The *falfe* appearance of a *greatnef* of mind, that was inferred from Diocleatian *refigning* the Empire is *alfo* taken *oft* by this Relation's; *fince* it is plain, that both Diocletian's Brain was turned, that he was forced to it; fo that his *Refignation* ws not the effect of his *Philofophy* but the Unnatural Ambition of his Son in Law Maximian.[34]

---

31 P.S. Davies, "The Origin and Purpose of the Persecution of AD 303," *The Journal of Theological Studies, New Series*, 1989, 66
32 https://www.ancient.eu/Diocletian
33 Gonzalez, *The Story of Christianity*, 120
34 Lactantius and Gilbert Barnet, *A Relation of the Death of the*

He would further entail how during the council Diocletian would use a diviner to consult with Apollo, he describes as an "enemy of the Christian Religion,"[35] in deciding to "put an end to this religion."[36]

Eusebius recalls the first edict in the succession to dismantle the church enforced 17 September 301 as,

Ordering the churches to be razed to their foundation, and the Scriptures to be put out of their existence by fire, and proclaiming that those who held positions of honor be disenfranchised, that household servants, if they clung to the profession of Christianity, be deprived of their freedom.[37]

The construct of the edict set out to accomplish what previous years of persecution failed to do – eliminate, not just the spread of Christianity, but strategically wipe out the religion altogether by dismantling any perceived internal and external power. Christian men in official positions would suffer the same fate irrespective of citizenship, all seen as traitors and enemies of the state, therefore stripped of civil rights and state protection.[38]

Though not a recognized religion, Christianity had made its mark in the empire, constructing places of worship. Flattening churches and destroying property would leave no place for devout followers to gather unless they should dare risk

---

Primitive Persecutors, (Amsterdam), preface
35 Lactantius and Barnet, *A Relation of the Death of the Primitive Persecutors,* 78
36 Lactantius and Barnet, *A Relation of the Death of the Primitive Persecutors,* 78
37 Eusebius and Defarrari, *Ecclesiastical History,* 167
38 Arthur James Mason, *The Persecution of Diocletian: A Historical Essay,* (Deighton Bell and Co,), 103

assembling in public spaces, resulting in torture or death. Furthermore, the same idea was used in forcing Patriarchs to denounce Christianity and make sacrifices to the gods. Ideally, the lack of bishops (those who would apostate or become imprisoned) also eliminated the assembly of Christians. Many in control of the churches contended to the empire's demands with torment yet, "...countless others growing numb of souls because of cowardice proved weak at the first attack."[39] Unfortunately, the issue of dealing with those who "lapsed" compared to those who became martyrs would become a major issue of resolute for the church in the years to come.

Diocletian, who came to fully believe Christians conspired to overthrow him, used all knowledge and understanding to dismantle the church, to include his awareness of division in the church. He would come to use such knowledge by pitting one side against the other, thereby creating schisms and heresy over doctrines and Scripture.[40] The issue of sound doctrine and filtering schisms and heresies would become, yet, another major resolve for the church in the years to come.

Diocletian's second edict would become the darkest period in persecutions for Christians. Accusing Christians of setting fires in the imperial palace and further conspiracies, Diocletian would follow the persecutions set years before by Decius.[41] The list of martyrs would continue to grow without end. Meanwhile, as torments worsened and those captured were mutilated, Eubeius, tells how many would attempt to avoid such trials by throwing, "...themselves down from high buildings, considering death as booty taken from the wicked-

---

[39] Eusebius and Defarrari, *Ecclesiastical History*, 168
[40] Mason, *The Persecution of Diocletian*, 110
[41] Gonzalez, *The Story of Christianity*, 121

ness of evil men."[42]

Christianity had faced it greatest challenges in what Eusebius calls, "the darkest and most gloomy night"[43] before happiness and peace were reestablished in the public affairs of the Roman government and "ancestral goodwill toward each other was revived." The historian recalls the government dividing against itself, after a change in emperors, resulting in a civil war, which ultimately ended in peace through the empire. The era of peace would change the dynamics of the previous church-state relationship in years, also giving way to a new era for the future of the church.

Day Break – A New Era Dawns

The dawn of a new era in church-state relationships would evolve as Constantine was celebrated as Emperor of Rome. Eusebius credits Constantine (along with Licinius before losing "losing his mind") as "being stirred up against the two most impious tyrants by God, the absolute Ruler."[44] His words to describe God and use of Constantine could also relate to previous emperors longing desire for the empire to worship them in their rule. Constantine, along with Licinius, is also referred to an honored and intelligent piety[45] compared to predecessors such as Diocletian, noted as easily persuaded. Unlike his predecessors, Constantine would also credit his victory in the war, to the God the Christians worshipped.

Constantine's time as emperor and actions of working with the church had a profound impact on both Christianity and the Roman Empire, affecting what Christianity has evolved

---

42 Eusebius and Defarrari, *Ecclesiastical History*, 145
43 Eusebius and Defarrari, *Ecclesiastical History*,
44 Eusebius and Defarrari, *Ecclesiastical History*, 223-4
45 Eusebius and Defarrari, *Ecclesiastical History*, 229

to today. His diplomatic approach compared to his predecessors' tyrannical approach would begin to reshape Rome and the church. With Constantine at the helm, initially with Licinius, Christians would move from being outcasted and persecuted with little to no rights, to having all rights, and property reinstated, and Christianity recognized as a tolerable religion. His actions were opposite to the beliefs of his predecessors who believed and held Christians responsible for social and prosperous disruption, based on their teachings and practices. It is vital to note that while Constantine would give Christians the right to worship freely, he would not legalize the religion,[46] he also came to profess.

In 313, Constantine enacted the Edict of Milan, which officially extended freedom of worship to Christians,[47] but it was not until years later that Christianity would become the legal religion of the empire under the reign of Theodosius I. Though in the edict of Milan, the state would remain neutral in the affairs of the church, the edict designated the return of all church property seized during the persecution of Diocletian indicating the religion was important enough to need suitable places of worship. Furthermore, while not a legalized religion, Constantine and Licinius believed this act would provide favor of any god that the people in the empire prayed,[48] a belief differing than previous emperors. Perhaps, these same measures prompted his self-appointment to interfere in the affairs of the church, though having a positive

---

[46] Sidney Ehler and John Morral, *Church and state throughout the centuries: a collection of historic documents with commentaries* (London: Burns & Oats, 1954), 4

[47] Frederick Norris, Michael McHugh, and Everett Ferguson, *Encyclopedia of Early Church, vol 1, A-K* (New York: Garland Publishing, Inc, 1997), 257

[48] Ehler and Morral, *Church and State throughout the centuries*, 5

impact on the church.

In 314 and 325, Constantine, claiming duties as pontiff, would call a council in an attempt to resolve divisions over theology, a far cry from Diocletian who used heresy as a dismantling tool. At the time issues of schisms and heresy in the church caused ultimate disruptions. Bishops were attacking one another, populations were revolting against others, and men were committing sacrilegious acts.[49] The 314 Council of Arles would attempt to address the Donatist controversy in Western Rome, while the Council at Nicaea (325) would become the most noted and impactful council, for the church today. Here the ecclesiastical structure/teachings on foundation such as church order, governance, mission, and authority were established, along with a dedication to the "liberty and autonomy of the church" in its relationship with the state.[50] Eusebius exclaims the result of this First Ecumenical Council, was that the bishops of the nations were not only united concerning the faith but also agreed on the "celebration of the salutary feast of Easter." Thus, with all signatures committed, the emperor believed he obtained "a second victory over the adversary of the Church."[51]

Another issue the council would come to discuss was the matter of readmission (to the church) for those who "lapsed" during the persecution.[52] Unfortunately, this resolute would become ignored. The emperor's attempt to stop the quarrels amongst the bishops proved challenging. At the end of the

---

49 Eusebius, *Life of Constantine,* (Oxford: Oxford University Press, 1999), 122

50 Norris, McHugh, and Ferguson, *Encyclopedia of Early Church,* 257-8

51 Eusebius, *Life of Constantine,* 127

52 Gonzalez, *The Story of Christianity,* 187

First Ecumenical Council, he encourages them to avoid contentious quarrels and be tolerant.[53] Unfortunately, he would need to repeat the summons as mutual bitterness remained.[54]

In the Constantinople era, as persecutions are no longer tolerated and the church moves to become the favored church, with the state, it would obtain advances in the areas of finance, art and construction. The church would be granted money to defray expenses[55] and clergy the exemption from political duties. This exemption would prevent clergy from being drawn away from services to the Deity without hindrance to the law. Such a benefit, the entire empire was thought to prosper from.[56]

The Emperor's construction projects would become admired pieces of church history. Constantine, himself, ordered the development of a place of worship, for the Savior, in connection with Jerusalem. He would ultimately build the "three most Sacred sites:"[57] Church of the Holy Sepulcher,[58] and the Churches at Bethlehem and Accession, to bestow honor to the Savior.[59] Other churches were established throughout the provinces making them "far higher than public esteem" and the city that would bear Constantine's name, he also embellished with many places of worship and tombs of martyrs, purging places of idol worship and foul alters.[60]

---

53 Eusebius, *Life of Constantine,* 131
54 Eusebius, *Life of Constantine,* 132
55 Eusebius, *Life of Constantine,* 278
56 Eusebius, *Life of Constantine,* 280
57 Eusebius, *Life of Constantine,* 132
58 Eusebius, *Life of Constantine,* 133
59 Eusebius, *Life of Constantine,* 137
60 Eusebius, *Life of Constantine,* 140

While the church would reap many benefits, for years to come, in its new relationship with the state, so would the remainder of the empire. Persecutory emperors always believed that those proclaiming Christianity were to blame for any demise of the empire, yet once the persecutions ended and a new relationship was established, it would seem the entire empire would benefit from this new relationship. Constantine would "plan for the happiness of mankind." In one example, holding today was "the removal of one-fourth of the annual tax charge" on land and allowed this to landlords, so one collecting the annual deductible was not liable.[61] Being politically astute, he would accomplish what was nearly impossible for his prior colleagues: getting the Barbarians to subject to Roman Rule.[62]

The noted end of an era was the beginning of change that became vital to the future. The development and use of theology, enriched in the Nicene Creeds, the celebratory of Easter, and countless pilgrimages to visit places such as the Church of the Holy Selchupue, are reminders of the formation of the church, the richness of its history, and the cost of its development for the people and an empire.

What becomes most interesting in examining the reasons behind the persecutions, pertaining to the church-state relationship, are the misguided fears of those in charge. Emperors, charged with the welfare of an empire, understood the value of loyalty and unity in the kingdom for it to thrive, yet failed to comprehend or believe the values and teachings of those within the empire. These undervalued teachings and practices, rather than becoming included in a system, were blamed for the demise of the empire, thus often led to the

---

61 Eusebius, *Life of Constantine,* 154
62 Eusebius, *Life of Constantine,* 155

persecution of those belonging to the church and the desecration of church property. Interestingly enough, four centuries later, an emperor, would assume the throne, yet with a totally different view. Rather than fearing and persecuting the church, he would come to favor it. Thus what others felt as what was cause for wiping out the church, Constantine used for building relationships, resulting in benefits for the entire empire.

Willie James Jennings uses A Theological Commentary on the Bible: Acts, to help the church struggling with individualism to understand that the book of Acts is not just a historical reference, but a theological reference offering instruction in historical consciousness to deal with today's issues.[63] Jennings draws the reader's attention to the tension surrounding the diaspora of Israel and the Roman Empire, with God's intervention to join these lives, offering a new world. As he spells out, God's intervention would disrupt individual fundamental ideas of nationalism, socialism, and economics reconstructing them to shared "stories bound to a new destiny in God." [64]

Through Acts, Jennings explains that as God moves, changing the perception of the diaspora of isolation to connecting with God, we are called to open ourselves to action.[65] This would imply that as God moves, a demand is placed that requires a response in which one "yields" to the altercation of faith received joining God's body, therefore open to others joining the body later.[66] The authority by which one yields to is no longer their own, which could be motivated by fear of loss of identity, but that of the Holy Spirit. Thus, allowing

---

63 (Jennings 2017), 2
64 (Jennings 2017), 11
65 (Jennings 2017), 13
66 (Jennings 2017), 37

the reconstruction of social order which expands the kingdom, rather than allowing one to lose identity. In this reconstructed social order, new desires and values are formed in which we extend our boundaries into new spaces becoming conjoined with "people, the surroundings, the animals, and the ground itself."[67] The community becomes redefined.

Jennings challenges the reader's perspective, based on westernized church teachings, by retelling the violent death of Ananias and Sapphira, to demonstrate God's action to unify and restructure community.[68] In this new order, possessions and money would no longer establish and divide social hierarchies. Furthermore, in the establishment of order, God's actions towards their offense would repel Israel's old systems of killings for crimes. Jennings points out that new cultural, social, and economic boundaries were constructed, especially the understanding that the couple belongs to a greater community, rather than in insolation belonging only to themselves.[69]

Jennings storytelling of the life of Paul underscores the lessons of socialism and nationalism as we see the tension undergirded in Paul's suffering from persecution and judgment in Acts 21-28. A Jew and Roman Citizen, yet a convert of the Way, the tension unfolds around perceived crimes and Paul's "rightful" judge. Connecting back to Jennings' discussion on God's actions to reform social order, he identifies at least two issues God has confronted in understanding the authoritative structure, in previous chapters of Acts: of Christ as

---

67 (Jennings 2017), 249
68 (Jennings, 2017), 53
69 (Jennings, 2017), 54

judge[70] and yielding to the Spirit to invite others to the body.[71] The author's form of storytelling demonstrates the tension and anguish of diaspora in Paul's journey as the reader is shown results of not yielding to authority, instead allowing fear to rule as judgment. Through Jennings commentary, we witness a historical Acts played out in present Acts, which Jennings will further point to relevance in the reader's current issues, such as the church's struggle with reaching beyond physical communal boundaries.[72]

I appreciate how Jennings describes Paul as representing an alternative vision of joining in which Jew and Gentile found each other at the resurrected body of Jesus Christ.[73] It is the reflection of two opposite sides coming to understand that they can come together without fear of losing themselves. The idea Jennings presents, in Acts, that joining together would not cause one side to lose themselves, but would expand the kingdom is perhaps a thought not considered often enough. I would agree that our lives are fragmented based on the lines we have created geographically, culturally, economically, and emotionally instead of then seeing the value of living a shared life. Rather than yielding and following God to understand community, we have defined community and neighbor based our paradigm. This creates the tension we see witnessed in the life of Paul caused by the diaspora of both of his people- Jews and Romans.[74] (199-202). This is same tension, Jennings identified at the beginning of Acts that God moved to confront and dismantle.

---

70 (Jennings, 2017), 47

71 (Jennings, 2017), 37

72 (Jennings, 2017), 250

73 (Jennings, 201t), 222

74 (Jennings, 2017), 199-202

Removing Boundaries and Limitations

Is it possible that two distinct groups of people can see God differently, yet realize they worship the same God? Can we begin to see the commonalities of our beliefs rather than focus on the differences, in order to pursue peaceful relationships? In Allah, A Christian Response, Miroslav Volf takes on these challenging questions. He explores the religions of Muslims and Christians, inviting readers to see "truth," "with the eyes of inviting and reconciling love," rather than truth" born of cold indifference or simmering hate."[75]

The author uses the events surrounding President Obama's 2009 inauguration to introduce the reader to the discourse between the groups yet shedding light on the impending possibility that perhaps there is unnecessary friction. He tells of the public outcry and accusations of blasphemy against Rick Warren's inaugural prayer. Warren was accused of identifying the "deities of Christianity and Islam as one in the same."[76] He implies that the argument that we do not worship the same God is "encrusted" in emotionally charged negative stereotypes and ideologies rather than truth.[77]

Throughout the novel, Volf explores various ideas, dispelling myths, and shedding light on influences that fuel the animos-

---

75 (Volf 2011), 16
76 Volf 2011), 6
77 (Volf 2011), 16

ity between these groups. An interesting point he explores is the historical influences of "ancient grievances," as he called them, behind the tensions and if they, in fact, have to deal with religion or other issues. He points out that our "memories disturb the peace of the present." [78] We must understand the hurt in order to heal.[79]

These points are important because if we wish to move forward in reconciliation, then we must first understand what is "broken." The core of the argument seems not just about the God we worship but the actions of those who worship the God we believe in. The traumatic events of the Twin towers, as the author notes, caused the heightened (curiosity) from Christians regarding the differentiation of God. Though the author argues the challenges Islam faces with the accusation of being a violent religion, he graciously reminds us of the violence in Christian history as well, again shedding light on similarities. I, however, would argue the similarity of false persecution and the importance of seeking "truth."

Plantinga et al. reminds us of the years of persecution faced by Christians based on a lack of understanding of practices. Early apologists, such as Athenagoras, defended Christians on false accusations of cannibalism and false worship. These accusations were in part due to misconceptions regarding the Christian faith and practices.[80] Not only did it take Athenagoras to speak, but it took the emperor to listen, eventually granting religious toleration and protection to Christianity. Our lesson is to look at history and see God working, then apply it to our current life and decisions.

---

78 (Volf 2011), 3
79 (Volf 2011), 2
80 (Plantinga, Thompson and Lundberg 2010) 424-425

From the perspective of the Christian Church, it would seem important to transform our ideas and thoughts in hope to better understand the views of other human beings. Willard would imply to embrace the discipline of "study." The more we study, not only the word of God but, in this case, our history, it allows God to meet with and speak specifically to us.[81] In turn, we become better empowered by God and distributed through society appropriately[82] rather than moving forward independently and possibly adding more wrath in the earth.

Volf denies that Muslims and Christians worship a different god, but the way each group worships may differ. In this case, he implies that "a common God nudges people to actually employ those common values to set aside animosities."[83] I am inclined to agree with this statement. The "nudge" would be William Ladd's idea that the kingdom of God places a demand on us to embody the kingdom in our decisions and everyday life. It is important to respond to God with a resolute decision to follow him. While it is understandable that events from the past can cause hurt and distrust, through God's Word, we can see him at work. As we make the resolute, irrevocable, and clean-cut decision[84] to follow Christ, we are realizing we can no longer "cling to the past." Instead, we are moving forward to embrace, receive, and cooperate with God in redeeming the kingdom. It is only then we can begin to receive the blessings and destiny reserved for those who embrace God's Kingdom.[85]

---

81 (Willard 1991), 176-177
82 (Willard 1991), 231
83 (Volf 2011), 9
84 (Ladd 1959), 99
85 (Ladd 1959), 99

The greatest challenge posed by Volf was the idea of embracing pluralism.[86] Initially, it seemed the idea was quite contrary to everything he previously discussed regarding respecting the differences and embracing the commonalities without forcing the ways of one on another. Each faith group believes they are the only true religion, taking its laws of the land infused with personal values embodied with God's commands, to govern their lives and communities.[87] In essence, the identity of each group is formed from religion based on land, structures, and culture, as opposed to God.

There are pros and cons to this challenge. Ideally, it would seem radical to imagine a world where we focused solely on our identity from God rather than religious structures, land, etc. I would agree, we would be more inclined to focus on our "allegiance to God who commands love of neighbor" and nudge our actions in caring for others.[88] Yes, we would begin to embrace our commonalities more, which is great in theory. The challenge becomes the possibility of overlooking the differences. While each group does share commonalities, we cannot negate the Great Commission to go forth and make disciples and spread the Gospel. Therefore, combining religions would not completely work. While people may "live" according to the commands of God, the absent element is still the "teachings" of Christ. Yes, some aspect of teaching is possible by demonstration. When done fully, as Willard implies, "evangelism will be unstoppable and largely automatic" where the local assembly would become an academy to learn how to live.[89]

---

86 (Volf, 2011), 224
87 (Volf, 2011), 224
88 (Volf 2011), 250
89 (Willard 1991), 247

Islam does not deny Jesus completely, though the belief differs significantly from those who follow Christianity. In this case, the religions cannot be combined, though each group of people ought to be respected. For instance, in chapter ten, Volf cleverly notes ways Christian beliefs differ, yet they are still "100 percent Christian." Quite an interesting approach when he explains the attributes that make each group exclusivists; each claiming they worship the only TRUE GOD. If these attributes or characteristics differ vastly across Christian faith groups, yet there is little to no animosity, then why can we not extend the same grace across other faith groups?

Jonathan Sacks stated that "it is a faith in which God invites human beings to become his partners in the work of redemption; to build a society on the basis of a justice that people understand as such; a human world, without hubris (the attempt to be more than human) or nemesis (a descent into the less than human)."[90] To work with God and make the ultimate change, individual change is the key.[91] Christians often speak of the redeeming works of salvation, yet I wonder how often we have reflected upon what it means to be saved, by Christ. Knowing and understanding truth is not seeing the Bible through the eyes of the world but seeing the world through the eyes of the Bible, The Word of God. In essence, we are then able to live a life of salvation, being obedient to "...the Torah as definitively interpreted by Yeshua."[92] It is then we begin to understand what it means not just to be saved but work in the salvation of the kingdom.

---

90 (Rabbi Sacks 2005), 27
91 (Willard 1991), 237
92 (Kinnaman, You Lost Me: Why Young Christians Are Leaving The Church...And Rethinking Faith 2011), 126

God commands, in the Torah, we love our neighbor, Christ demonstrated or interpreted this in his teachings showing love to not just Jews but also Gentiles. Christ showed love, grace, and mercy to those in the community most would not show favor to, the outcasts, and even those who persecuted him. From this demonstration, today's church can take away a lesson on who is our neighbor. Our neighbor is not just the person that looks like us, dresses like us, worships or prays like us. Though each person is different, we are to love them. While there may be things in history that have caused hurt or distrust, as we embody the ways of Christ, we also learn forgiveness and understanding. Even as Jesus was on the cross, he asked God to forgive those who persecuted and berated him because they lacked understanding. As today's church, invited to partner with God in the work of redemption, we too, must look past the actions of those with lack of understanding by first gaining an understanding of the demands God places upon us. Finally, we must learn to respond appropriately, in truth guided by God, Jesus, and The Holy Spirit.

Karl Barth advised that we should "Take your Bible and take your newspaper, and read both. But interpret newspapers from your Bible." I would contend that we can look at this quote and apply it to our view of modern-day issues, but also see how our issues influence our theology.

As much we attempt to take a quality systematic theological approach in addressing modern day matters, we may very well uncover that we are more affected by anthropological influences than we care to accept. We are much like those who struggled, in the past, with how their upbringing, background, and influences helped formulate their ideas about God, thereby influencing how they engaged with the world around them. While our background and upbringing are important, we must also understand the complexity of this significance.

While we should always be evolving and aware of what is going on around us, we must also be aware of how we engage. The proper theological engagement with cultural, political, and social issues must happen not only within a church but also outside, as well. As we look, at both the historical and practical sub-discipline of systematic theology, we can see how we are influenced and developed to engage with others and why. In context, our theologies will teach us how to live and what we believe. In turn, we apply practical concepts to carry out our beliefs, as we address things like social issues. For instance, our historical theology may teach us to care for the poor (a social issue). The practical theology could be systematic of an anthropological issue resulting in who we see as poor and how we choose to help them, therefore, how we may actually address the social issue. The result could be overlooking those nearby that require a great deal of help or having a false sense of reality about those nearby that require help. My point is this. Sometimes, we may be quick to attack problems or issues in our day. Perhaps, Karl Barth would want us to take a step back to identify why we are addressing such matters the way we do. Are we doing so, according to doctrines, based on human feelings or "the utterance of God to humanity?"[93]

God will use our life to refine us, or we can allow it to define us. Unfortunately, as some would come to Christ, and their life would become transformed, some would continue to struggle in their perspective of God. We can read the Bible learning stories of wondrous works the Lord performed, yet

---

93 (Plantinga, Thompson and Lundberg 2010), 11

somehow, we still struggle in believing the same God exists and operates the same today. This struggle became aspects of our practices and religious traditions. We read the Word of God through our background rather than understanding the background of the Word. With the former view, we could begin to apply the word to our life by hearing God speak to us rather than allowing our life to speak to the Word. This would give a greater meaning to understanding how the Bible is the Living Word of God. Unfortunately, reading the Bible through our lives form our narrow and humanistic view of God and becomes the distorted image we pass along to those we encounter. It distorts the image of God for those He is calling to develop a relationship with Him.

People practice a faith that discard the mystical and supernatural yet believe in the supernatural God. It is not that God cannot perform such acts as we read about in the Bible, the problem lies in what humans struggle to believe. The tension in faith is the struggle between sociological and anthropological backgrounds and the transformation we must discipline ourselves in our walk with Christ. Spiritual disciplines help transform our beliefs beyond the confines of a humanistic image of God that has limitations. I would argue that one of the greatest challenges we have is we have formed God in our image rather than realizing we were formed in the image and likeness of God. The image in which we create becomes the hinderance in accepting the mystical God as we see Him through our human limitations. Even in religion, doctrines were formed as men had difficulties accepting a mystical God. Throughout religious history, we can find the documented trouble and confusion of religious fathers accepting ideals that were too mystical, therefore documenting them as emotional or undisciplined. Therefore, the theologies with restraints and limitations on God were passed on and down for generations. How can one have an encounter and continued walk with God, yet their view or perspective remains unchanged?

As you continue to walk your journey through life, you will witness, experience, and encounter different people, opportunities, and situations. Sometimes we will miss certain opportunities and connections because we are accustomed to seeing things a certain way. Our thoughts and views are limited, based on what we have been trained to see or have trained our eyes and heart to see. It is difficult to see something greater because we see through our eyes and not the eyes of God. So, if there is an opportunity to make connections or achieve greater things, we pass them by. When we have had an encounter with God, our life changes and continues to do so as we continue to walk with Him. A transformation happens as we are cleansed, drawn closer, get to know Him, worship Him, and establish a true connection with Him. Through this transformation, there is no way we should continue to see things as they were before. There is no way you should encounter people and situations as before.

Your connection should allow you to see as God sees. Looking at the world, experiences, and encounters with others should become new as you see through the heart and eyes of The Father. You no longer disregard what is different, but you began to embrace a different understanding. This allows you to make connections where God leads to better your life. You realize the difference between walking alone and with a transformed mind with Christ.

Christ came to redeem us all, so why do we disregard those with differences? Why do we miss opportunities for greatness? Why are we always looking for more but never find it? Because we fail to become changed…transformed and walk through life with God, seeing the world as He does.

For way too long in this country, arguments of racism and immigration, have stood in the forefront. Have we moved forward, or are we static in relationships? How have we evolved, but most importantly, are we abiding by ethical Christian standards in relationships with others? Has a country that has a Statue of Liberty with the inscription: "Give me your tired, your poor, Your huddled masses **yearning** to breathe free, The **wretched** refuse of your teeming shore," have we lived these words or have we applied a different set of ethical standards that include some but excludes others? If so, how does this align with what we believe Christian ethics should reflect?

Can the oppressed become the oppressor? In an attempt to gain freedom, is it possible for people to forget their own journey, therefore becoming everything they originally fought against? Fighting for a way to escape a life of religious persecution, initial settlers made their way to this country. Kept from the ability to thrive through religion and economics, this land was a means to escape and find freedom.

Similar to those who were oppressed by the pharaoh, led and guided to a faraway land for freedom and the promise of God, could this have been the promise land for the Europeans? Did they have a similar plight as the Israelite to include levels of disobedience and apostasy, ultimately receiving warnings from God for their failure to take care of others in need as God had taken care of them?

A country built upon immigration, its people, have created a blockage for those who seek to migrate and take refuge in their promise land. With the initiation of immigration laws (reforms), it seems that the original sin of America is still the great sin of America.

Two major border points continue to be the focus of American Immigration concerns and arguments. Those entering from across the water from the east and from all areas of the south. This is not to negate that other entry points exist, but when examining two somewhat specific points, we will begin to notice a pattern of how people are received and treated. This treatment of inclusion and exclusion is the primary focus of Christian Ethical Behavior/response toward those in need. Let's examine the initial entry points of those who traveled from eastern parts of the world seeking refuge and the evolving response to others who sought the same but denied. In turn, we can highlight current concerns and points of view that could make room for better relationships, based on Christian Principles.

Immigration Evolution and Race Structure

In examining the evolution of immigration in America, it is interesting that we are reminded that the majority of the first "immigrants" hailed from Northern and Western Europe. These individuals left their homes, giving up everything to seek a better life. Starting with those who fled from religious persecution and desiring religious freedom, to those who were completely impoverished and seeking new opportunities, people made the voyage to their land of opportunity and promise. For over two centuries, this would continue as new lives were created and the initial persons who came would not be known as immigrants but as pilgrims.

A pilgrim, according to dictionary.com, is one who journeys, especially a long distance, to some sacred place as an act of religious devotion. They are also known as travelers or wanders in a foreign place. Interestingly enough, those outside of this original community would come to be known as immigrants. Immigrants have a much different meaning. They are people who come to live permanently in a foreign land. They are NOT natives but here, in America, those who first sought refuge here were also not natives. In true definition, they were immigrants. These immigrants would become the very people who would later form laws/rules to keep others from coming to this country to seek the same freedoms they did.

In 1882, the Chinese Exclusion Act became the first significant legislation restricting immigration.[94] Seeking new opportunities during the gold rush, Chinese laborers were banned by the original immigrants, predominantly the Anglo-Saxon Protestant population. The justification for the act was that new laborers were seen as unwanted competition for jobs. The Irish, at the time, were also experiencing discrimination for their religious beliefs.

A very systematic race structure has evolved from the laws of immigration. Within this structure exists the means to oppress the disenfranchised, making fewer opportunities available, and a system that supports mostly or only the privileged. Meanwhile, those who are marginalized have become victims of dehumanization and depravity. This evolvement has also become evident in early reforms in which quota laws were enacted favoring European immigrants. Although these laws were eliminated, behaviors still were evidenced, as those who seek refuge from non-European countries, today face less scrutiny entering U.S. Borders. According to the US Library of Congress, most of these immigrants enter through the east coast, where the Statue of Liberty stands, "welcoming" the "huddled masses yearning to breathe free" to the United States. As part of the privileged community, the majority of Europeans immigrants are able to receive permanent residence status in the US as immediate relatives of US Citizens or through employment channels. Interestingly

---

94 History.com Staff, U.S. Immigration Before 1965, http://www.history.com/topics/u-s-immigration-before-1965, (2009)

enough, these immigrants, compared to the overall foreign and native-born populations, are less likely to participate in the labor force.[95]

On the other hand, those coming from more impoverished areas, seeking opportunities such as employment, and freedom from persecution, war, and injustices in their home, are most likely rejected and denied opportunity. Most live in a state of instability and fear of deportation. Most arguments on the news are opposing their access to the pursuit of happiness or the ability to be welcomed according to the words on Lady Liberty. In fact, most of these disfranchised individuals are greeted by border signs that warn them of entering illegally. How can we welcome those who can afford to fly here and possibly live comfortably with the light of the Statue of Liberty but those who struggle and may be on the brink of losing their very life, are greeted by the security that will most likely lock them up and/or send them home? This is a far contrast to the initial entrance of those who scraped to escape, seeking freedom in a new land over three centuries ago. Where is the justice? What type of ethical morals are we living by? As a nation founded upon the ideals of immigration, how do we begin to move back to those very same principles to no longer have a society of privileged vs. disenfranchised?

Ethical Reasoning

Authors Traci West, in <u>Disruptive Christian Ethics,</u> and Miguel A. De La Torre, in <u>Doing Christian Ethics From the Margins</u>, take very different approaches to deal with the marginalized in this country. While both would argue that a

---

[95] Jie Zong and Jeanne Batalova, European Immigrants in the United States, http://www.migrationpolicy.org/article/european-immigrants-united-states, (1 December 2015)

change is necessary to advance the oppressed to liberation, their methods of ethical view on getting there differ.

De La Torre's argument that Christian ethics from the center reflects the thoughts of the dominant culture in the center. Here the marginalized interpret reality through the eyes of their oppressor, resulting in a degrading form of humility. Yet, it is not the marginalized who must be humbled. The author sees the privileged as ones who must understand humility and acknowledge their sinful and proud ways. He goes on to discuss that while Christian identity hinges upon grace, this has been perverted by those who are privileged.

Grace has become a means by which a doctrine of forgiveness and reconciliation with God becomes so prominent that change takes a backseat (or becomes non-existent). All become forgiven without converting from practices that allow oppressive behavior or structures. He points out the dangers of justification as taught by Jesus. The belief is that works of faith become the excuse to rely upon. The notion of, "I am participating in liturgical practices, therefore, all is well," but in truth, one ignores things like being concerned with the disenfranchised.

The concern for the disenfranchised has been a principle that God has emphasized since the beginning of time. In teaching the Israelites to learn to live in covenant with Him, God continuously reminded His people the importance of taking care of the marginalized or helpless. In Isaiah 1, God sent the prophet to the Israelites with words of warning and judgment for living as De La Torre calls "Sola Fide." The Israelites were considered and called a sinful nation as they were still keeping with their religious practices and sacrifices, yet they too failed to "rescue the oppressed, defend the orphan, and plead for the widow." A call for a change or face consequences was imminent.

De La Torre's views would align with the message of change of character, therefore, fitting the ethical reasoning of virtue. This is in vast contrast to the reasoning of Traci West. West believes that practices of ethics should derive from shared concrete communal practices. The idea is that all have an obligation to participate, therefore, resulting in a positive outcome of human rights, as defined by Deontological Reasoning. West further explains that the tools required for social change are found in the "core elements of Christianity, such as scripture, worship, and church ministerial leadership."[96]

More Than One Right Way

In examining the current situation of race and structure in immigration, along with the viewpoints of both West and De La Torre, I believe they are both valid but are missing elements in their argument. De La Torre, while he emphasizes the need for individual character change, that change, is loosely based on an obligation to follow Christian laws. De La Torre mentions the foundations of Christ's ministry, but the prominent idea of that foundation is in Christ's favor toward the marginalized. This only gives way to keeping the distinguishing lines of the privileged and marginalized. Based on this argument, I contend that even if individual characteristics change, the underlying issue was the existence of a structure that will not be changed. The structure must become the foundation that is based on Biblical principles, such as the call in Isaiah 1. While God's message was for change, it was based on understanding the established covenant. The change would have been in response to understanding the obligation to live a certain way.

---

96 Traci West, Disruptive Christian Ethics, (Louisville: Westminster John Knox Press, 2006)

West, on the other hand, focuses on the need to follow the "rules" yet her view of established theory and practice together is somewhat flowery. I agree that the two must coexist, but unless character change is present, true progression will not happen. Aspects of De La Torre's argument and reasoning could be combined with that of West's. Rather than two separate reasonings, perhaps, the change we need is our response to our Christian obligations/duty.

In this new combined reasoning or approach, we must remember, as a nation, our journey from being marginalized to liberated. As a land in which people came to find hope, peace, and freedom much like the Israelites seeking refuge, Americans must not take this liberation for granted and continue on with this the utilitarian idea, therefore, believing something is being protected by denying others. Instead, the response should be the same that God tried to teach the Israelites during their deliverance and journey. The message in Exodus 22:21-22 is to "not wrong or oppress a resident alien, for you were aliens in the land of Egypt. You shall not abuse any widow or orphan." This is repeated again in Exodus 23:9, "You shall not oppress a resident alien: you know the heart of an alien for you were aliens in the land of Egypt." These concerns, along with other social concerns, were addressed in the covenant in the Old Testament. Concerns such as the importance of safeguarding the dignity and rights of people and that no one should be powerless, exploited, or impoverished were addressed in establishing a covenant.

My thought is that once we return to learning to follow some of the same laws that were established in the covenant (initial learning to live with God), then we begin to move towards embracing the ministry of Jesus. Through this embracement is where change can begin rather than living under hyper-graced theological practices, as described by De La Torre. It is here that we began to acknowledge the similarities and dissimilarities of people, therefore, learning to welcome new residents with empathy and compassion forming true cross-cultural relationships. Ultimately this allows us to reach a place where new/improved structural systems are in place and not ones which deny true freedoms for all.

Researchers believe that the in part, a person's identity is derived from their social identity.[97] In social identity theory, a person knows they belong to a particular social category or group based on a shared identity, such as race, ethnic, group, or religion. Unfortunately, social identities become identity contingencies[98] having an adverse effect on a person's life, especially when individuals are judged on their social identity rather than their individual identity.

Identity contingencies, or life conditions tied to a person's social identity, become circumstances they must deal with in order to get what they want or need in a situation.[99] These presented conditions become the primary focus, therefore exhausting a person's energy making it more difficult to achieve their goals. Focused on defeating the stereotype, working to disprove how others may see them, the individual is unable to live as themselves freely. Who they are is tied to the way others see them.[100] The person ultimately finds themselves

---

[97] Jan E. Stets and Peter J. Burke. "Identity Theory and Social Theory." *Social Psychology Quarterly,* 2000, 224

[98] Claude M. Steel, *Whistling Vivaldi: How Stereotypes Affect Us and What We Can Do* (New York: W.W. Norton, 2010), 3

[99] Steele, *Whistling Vivaldi,* 3

[100] Brian Bantum. *The Death of Race: Building a New Christianity in a Racial World* (Minneapolis: Augsburg Fortress Publishers,

caught between questions of who others say they are, who they believe they are, and who they will come to be.[101]

Let's explore the challenges of living beyond stereotypes tied to a person's social identity, affecting one's ability to achieve their goal. Though, unconventional and arduous to do, I will use myself as a case study, sharing my experience at a predominantly white evangelical seminary. I will study this case through the foundational lens of three primary works: Claude Steele's, *Whistling Vivaldi*, Jane Elliott's social exercise "Blue Eyes/Brown Eyes," and Willie James Jennings' *Acts*. These works along with the case study, will highlight aspects of stereotype threats and their impact on social identity as well as provide insight on how we can create environments for humanity to live in their full identity, as they see themselves, therefore becoming bridges that bring us together, giving hope for a shared life, open cultural, familiar and tribal alliances and allegiances.[102]

In *Whistling Vivaldi*, Claude Steel demonstrates how stereotypes, or identity contingencies, shape and threaten how we feel about ourselves and who we hope to be.[103] He explores these stereotype threats and their contributions to vexing personal and societal problems in hopes to reduce such threats, therefore leading to dramatic improvements in these problems.[104] Steele identifies three ways by which these threats become damaging. They make a difference in how we perform in certain situations to the careers and friend

---

2016), 24
101 Bantum, *The Death of Race*, 129
102 Willie James Jennings, *Acts* (Louisville: Westminster John Knox Press, 2017), 88
103 Steele, *Whistling Vivaldi*, 14
104 Steele, *Whistling Vivaldi*, 11

and friends we choose; affect social problems that range from racial and social class and gender achievements gaps that distort intergroup tensions troubling social relations; and impairment of human functioning.[105]

Steele explains how identity contingencies that made the biggest difference in our functioning can threaten or restrict us in some way.[106] Even as we have complex identities, what we understand as being attacked in the moment, becomes they are so powerful making us aware of being a particular "kind of person."[107] These adverse contingencies become preoccupying, therefore, shaping how we perform or function and becomes more important than any other identities, for the time.[108]

To further explore how these contingencies, affect our functioning, he describes a student, who reached out to him telling how she enjoyed his lecture on social identities. He recalls the nine social identities listed on a Powerpoint slide to include age, sex, sexual orientation, race, profession, nationality, and political affiliation.[109] While the student states that mental health status was not mentioned, she identifies as having bipolar disorder, therefore, could relate to the threats Steele discusses in his lecture. The student feared publicly asking a question during the lecture based on how she would be perceived or discriminated against based on other's biases. She believed this could lead to greater implications such as embarrassment, social rejection, loss of career opportunities, being judged or dismissed. Steele states the student lives remaining cognizant of her social world constantly mindful of

---

105 Steele, *Whistling Vivaldi*, 14-15
106 Steele, *Whistling Vivaldi*, 66
107 Steele, *Whistling Vivaldi*, 73
108 Steele, *Whistling Vivaldi*, 71-72
109 Steele, *Whistling Vivaldi*, 70

how others feel about people who are bipolar (or this social group).[110]

Stereotypes can pose various forms of threats, such as the pressure to not conform to threats, especially those rooted in situational contingencies.[111] In his research, students were observed under the effects of stereotype threats, to determine how the threat interfered with performance.[112] They realized that a mind working to defeat a stereotype leaves little mental capacity free for anything else we are doing.[113]

To overcome stereotypes, we must be vigilant to possible contingencies to create identity integration settings.[114] This means people must be willing to confront identity threats to create identity-integrated situations where people do not have to cope with tasks of situations protecting themselves from the risk of being negatively judged and treated.[115] Instead, people would feel safe from the risk of identity predicaments in identity-integrated settings[116] where they may focus on being themselves, fully embracing their multiple identities.[117] They could use those identities as a bridge to build relationships and as a symbol of hope[118] for endless possibilities.

Stereotype threats, even those muted or subtle, in addition

---

110 Steele, *Whistling Vivaldi*, 71
111 Steele, *Whistling Vivaldi*, 89
112 Steele, *Whistling Vivaldi*, 121
113 Steele, *Whistling Vivaldi*, 123
114 Steele, *Whistling Vivaldi*, 139
115 Steele, *Whistling Vivaldi*, 213
116 Steele, *Whistling Vivaldi*, 215
117 Steele, *Whistling Vivaldi*, 218
118 Steele, *Whistling Vivaldi*, 219

to their effects, can cause tension between people from different groups in society, therefore, resulting in segregated enclaves.[119] Steele emphasizes the importance of identifying identity threats to create integrated spaces. However, Jane Elliot's controversial "Blue Eyes/Brown Eyes" exercise conducted in Britain demonstrates what happens when people become reluctant to identify threats.

In Jane Elliott's Blue Eyes/Brown Eyes Exercise, Jane attempts to introduce participants to how it feels to be a minority by simulating a racist apartheid-style regime.[120] She has replicated this social exercise for over fifty years to identify social prejudices. Jane initially devised this controversial exercise in 1968, in response to Dr. Martin Luther King's assassination.[121] Her goal was to teach her, then, third-grade class the importance of Dr. King's work.[122] Over the years, she would continue to repeat this exercise in various forums as she also lectures on diversity and inclusion.[123]

In 2013, Jane conducted the exercise in Britain, starting with thirty willing participants. The moderator explains they will be at the mercy of Jane, the leader, and unaware of what to expect despite having all come for the same purpose. They are told the purpose is to participate in a psychological study. The exercise immediately begins, while participants are checking in, as they are segregated and exposed to different treatment based on their eye color. Blue-eyed participants are bullied and receive a collar. The collar acts as an

---

[119] Steele, *Whistling Vivaldi*, 193
[120] Critical Voices, "How Racist Are you? Jane Elliott's Blue Eyes/Brown Eyes Exercise" 2013, Accessed You Tube
[121] www.janeelliott.com
[122] Steele, *Whistling Vivaldi*, 26
[123] http://www.janeelliott.com

additional identifier, like a label, enhancing the method of segregation.

The brown-eyed people receive direct access to their seats in the main hall. Here they meet with Jane, who explains the purpose of the exercise. By injecting live racism, she hopes the people will not allow these things to happen to others in the future. She informs them of their ability to make a difference or affect change.[124] Fundamentally, though controversial, Jane's exercise attempts to do the hard work of identifying identity threats to improve the experience of identity integration in real life settings.[125]

Not all agree with her plan, as one brown-eyed participant remains resistant during the remainder of the exercise. Through discussions, interactions, and posed challenges, she implies how flawed the assumptions are regarding the blue-eyed group. While she shares one identity with members of this group, the woman does not share the contingencies others in her group have presented. Examining the details of the exercise along with some of Steele's arguments, the woman does not realize that even in this exercise, she has "passed." Passing is the ability to shed one identity and the contingencies that go along with it for another.[126] The change in identities and subsequent contingencies provide different opportunities allowing one to be met with different expectations,[127] therefore affecting one's behavior, performance, and outcomes. The woman's selected identity, for this exercise, neutralized the threats (or discrimination) she would have

---

124 Critical Voices, "How Racist Are You?" https://youtu.be/Nqv9k-3jbtYU
125 Steele, *Whistling Vivaldi*, 151
126 Steele, *Whistling Vivaldi*, 65
127 Steele, *Whistling Vivaldi*, 66

received if segregated by skin color. Instead, she was included in a group of mixed people, with the opportunity to share experiences to affect change, if only she were open to it. Instead, she would use the opportunity to skew the exercise making aspects invaluable.

During the exercise tensions further escalate as the "blue-eyed" become reluctant in acknowledging the identity threats of the brown-eyed people, therefore debate over their described social identity threats and experiences. Some participants become rather dismissive, refusing to attentively hear what is being shared. A few deflect by trivializing the experience and over-identifies with the identity threat, therefore, becoming the "victim" and insists that any problem the brown-eyed person has the brown-eyed person is responsible for rectifying.[128]

The challenge the blue-eyed people presented in identifying identity threat was they viewed them from an observer's perspective. From the observer's perspective, this group attempted to explain away the brown-eyed people's problems through their personal biases. Therefore, they emphasized the contingency outcomes/effects and emphasized what they believed caused the problems[129]- the actions or beliefs the brown-eyed people should change.

At one point, the moderator flashes another video where Jane conducted the same experiment in Australia. In this scene, we observe a lesson that applies to this video. Through a conversation with a blue-eyed participant, we gain insight into how conforming affects one's identity. The participant is "downtrodden," and Jane asks what this feeling "teaches" her.

---

128 https://youtu.be/Nqv9k3jbtYU
129 Steele, *Whistling Vivaldi*, 18

She replies that if she is on the "hot seat," then it is her fault. It tells her that she must conform to the way Jane wants her to be. Therefore, making the participant feel worthless and insignificant. It is best to take on the new identity and be what Jane wants her to be and not who she is. She realizes that this is how someone loses their self-being.[130]

The exercise lasted two hours with heated debates and non-compliant participants that could not see the value in the exercise. Though the opportunity presented to identify contingencies, negative stereotypes, and prejudices, unfortunately, some participants were not receptive to detecting cues for contingency threats. They missed an opportunity to build a bridge towards communal relationships.

It is important to embrace those who are different to set the stage for new possibilities for interaction and relationships [131] while allowing everyone to freely be themselves. This new space or communal life, Jennings argues, pushes against the grain of individualism that societies are deeply committed to.[132] He explains that throughout time, people have become more disconnected and fragmented, seeing our lives in pieces rather than in consumption. [133] Though Jennings uses this discussion on fragmentation to emphasize the need to rethink geographical spaces and hospitality, the same argument can be used in examining social identities and hospitality. [134]

Creating fragmented pieces within social identities affect how we see ourselves and others, therefore creating more ways to

---

130 https://youtu.be/Nqv9k3jbtYU
131 Jennings, *Acts*, 87
132 Jennings, *Acts*, 247
133 Jennings, *Acts*, 248
134 Jennings, *Acts*, 250-251

drive people apart, as it decreases shared space. Jennings attributes these problems with internalized individualism[135] and invites readers to confront the boundaries that challenge our ability to unify and restructure community. Through Paul's story, in the book of Acts, we see "the story of God who desires us and all of creation and will not release us to isolations, social, economic, cultural, religious, gendered, and geographic."[136] He notes that through Christ, communities are pressed together (inclusive of one another), without the expectation of denying or forgetting what shapes their identity.[137] Instead, we can see and use the story of the eunuch as an ecclesial practice where our lives are brought together capturing and celebrate our differences thereby making visible the consuming and redemptive power and love of God.[138]

Though Steele mentions different stereotype threats across various social identities, my experiences in seminary relate to his presented challenges. My case demonstrates the value of taking inventory of situational contingencies in order to create identity-integrated environments. Like those Steele includes in his research, my social identity has influenced how I see myself, and how I understand others perceive me. My identity markers according to Steele's presented list for social identity include, I am black (African-American), a woman, heterosexual, Christian (of Pentecostal/Charismatic faith), a retired (disabled) veteran, and 44 years of age. Individually the markers I listed, do not reflect how I identify or see myself. Instead, each one helps to shape my identity. My identity is also shaped by my experiences, intellect,

---

135 Jennings, *Acts,* 53
136 Jennings, *Acts,* 11
137 Jennings, *Acts,* 12
138 Jennings, *Acts,* 90

emotional life, relationships, geographical (and national context) and beliefs. These aspects are important to note, as over two years of seminary, they also become identity contingencies[139] affecting how I would stay mindful of how others, in my new community, felt about people who shared my social identities.[140]

Initially, I entered the institution without feeling anxious or threats. There were "cues about the institution's inclusiveness" as I understood it to value "the experiences of group diversity."[141] This played a factor in selecting the institution. My important diversity factors included race, gender, and the interdenominational population. Steele argues that identifying cues can affect a person's sense of belonging as well as performance, as it detects threats people may encounter early on.[142] These unanticipated threats would quickly surface, bringing questions of belonging and ultimately affect my performance.

Dynamics of classroom/academic settings and their perceived threats could be affected by both professors and students. If a provoking threat is consistently presented, a person devalued unsettling one's sense of competence and belonging.[143] This would become a factor during my nearly twenty-six-month enrollment as a student at this institution where most often I was either the only African American student in a class or placed in a group forum (for an online class). Initially, this was not an issue, however, based on moderated lessons and discussions, it presented challenges where racial stereotypes

---

139 Steele, *Whistling Vivaldi*, 70
140 Steele, *Whistling Vivaldi*, 71
141 Steele, *Whistling Vivaldi*, 141
142 Steele, *Whistling Vivaldi*, 143-144
143 Steele, *Whistling Vivaldi*, 173

would become more prevalent. Sometimes this would be ignited by the seemingly forced self-introductions, where professors request what I call "introduction by labels (or social identities)." Online classes require the same to include the uncomfortable video.

Always reluctant to participate wishing this was not a requirement I became like Steele's bipolar student wondering how she would be judged; the same thought comes to mind. Responses to presented questions all carried a stigma, especially without having content and conversation. The moderation of introductions supports the fragmented identities that already divide people, allowing us to match our labels or decide which ones we rather not favor.

Anything I mention has a contingency threat attached that will make it harder to overcome for the next ten weeks. In my "diverse" and inclusive seminary, I quickly discovered I was not as free to be myself as I thought I would be. The first night of class, I learned the threat that will cause the greatest attack on my identity over the next two years. It became the ambiguities on how to interpret my experiences[144] as a Charismatic/Pentecostal. It began my first night of school and lasted through almost my final night.

I already felt pressured by the obvious identity that is on my body I felt I must work hard to overcome. Now, I get to add to that as I must also overcome the contingencies of being Pentecostal. In classes some professors and students implied we are all a bunch of rowdy, rambunctious people, with disorderly services, extraordinarily loud music, ridiculous and unnecessarily long prayers, lack liturgy, people calling themselves apostles and prophets which is crazy and not theolog-

---

144 Steele, *Whistling Vivaldi*, 60

ically correct, too mystical, and most of all preach (or teach) without sound theology. I heard it all.

I agree with Steele's argument that "critical mass" makes a difference when faced with intense identity threats.[145] With critical mass, the minority is no longer uncomfortable as their social identity number increases to a particular number. In my case, discovering the critical mass regarding the Pentecostal identity threat, was not as easy as identifying another African American student. Unless someone speaks out and self-identifies, you feel on an island stressed and burdened. Other students were similar to the brown-eyed woman in Jane Elliott's video who "passed." Unlike myself, they were able to shed one identity for another to help ease contingencies. I, on the other hand, rarely presented counter-arguments to these mocking claims, in these "diverse" settings. If I did, I thought about how I would be perceived, after all, I am also an African American woman who is often stereotyped as "angry" or upset even in intellectual conversations. So, much like a gentleman in Jane Elliott's video explains, sometimes, it is best to just "play the game" (or know how to get along).[146] Therefore, I retreated, mostly to working extra hard to disprove the stereotype hanging over my head.[147]

The effects of the contingencies caused me to shift from the excitement of learning to focus on proving that I could keep up and learn the material. I refused to confirm the stereotype threat, however, this became exacerbating. Like the African-American students in Steele's study, I became the student retreating to isolation and long, countless hours of study, often losing sleep compiled with odd study habits sim-

---

145 Steele, *Whistling Vivaldi*, 135
146 https://youtu.be/Nqv9k3jbtYU
147 Steele, *Whistling Vivaldi*, 105

ply to prove I was not inferior.[148] The focus became obscured and many times, the task too overwhelming.

It became a daunting task to prove I could reach the invisible bar set before me, and it was not panning out. Too focused on disproving the threat,[149] some grades suffered, and the pressures eventually took a toll on me physically, affecting my well-being.[150] After taking ill, suffering from repeated Fibromyalgia flares, something had to change. Confronted with what I was willing to risk completing my education, I decided I would confront these "tenacious forms of identity threat"[151] and live free as I saw myself even if that meant being judged. This is not to say results always had a gleaming effect. The presumptions about my identities such as race, military service, and religious beliefs, did not go away simply because I decided to revert to embracing my complex identities.

This was an internal process I had to endure similar to Steel's self-affirmation theory. When a self-image threat presents, Steele explains how we can take the opportunity to "preempt the image- restoring rationalization" by taking a step back, take a breath, and affirm a larger valued sense of self.[152] He further explains how the larger image of self-integrity makes the provoking threat seem less probative; therefore the person feels less a need to rationalize it away.[153] Furthermore, similar to the apostle Paul, I had to come to understand my "desperate-citizenship."[154] This point is where, through Christ,

---

148 Steele, *Whistling Vivaldi*, 31
149 Steele, *Whistling Vivaldi*, 109
150 Steele, *Whistling Vivaldi*, 127
151 Steele, *Whistling Vivaldi*, 213
152 Steele, *Whistling Vivaldi*, 173
153 Steele, *Whistling Vivaldi*, 173
154 Jennings, *Acts*, 206

I would embrace the vulnerabilities and uncertainties that came with my identity. Things will not always go as I desire them to yet staying focused on who I am and what I am called to do, there lies hope. The affirming effects of stepping back to "self-affirmation" became apparent in future contingencies.

A professor I respect and share a social identity with lectured on the challenges of leadership and church. Listening carefully, also wondering if I will engage in conversation. It has been several weeks of class, and my participation has been quite limited for two reasons. One, I am a retired veteran. Having spent over twenty years in service with extensive leadership experience, the information presented makes perfect sense.

Furthermore, much of the information presented I learned early in my career, and due to my career, I was taught the same well before I retired. Second, I come from a family of church leaders that goes back several generations. Many are well known within certain societal structures. For me, I am listening intensely learning how the material applies to various churches positively and negatively. My learning experience may be different, therefore I do not speak much.

After hearing several of the challenges in the context of the conversation I mention most of the material is familiar and was used in the military, besides, we attend the same leadership training as major corporations. I also mention how the church could learn from the military. Very dismissing, the professor informs that well, unfortunately, they are two very different entities, implying it was impossible. I was shut down along with my experience considering I was supposed to be a valued part of the class. The professor's observer's perspective presented a barrier to something outside of his bias. The two entities have more in common than he was willing to realize. I also wondered how he could easily dismiss my comment taking in consideration what he was teaching I explained how we taught the same material in the military. Why did this not spark interest? Rather than allowing his bias to devalue my self-identity, I was able to move on realizing the issue lied with him, not me.

I believe, this example also cuts to the core of one of Steele's arguments. These are the cues Steele points out that we must be vigilant of as we seek to create identity-integrated environments and neutral threats. The resistance lies in our receptiveness to these cues. Like the woman in the Britain video, we cannot express the need for inclusivity yet continue behaviors that enforce exclusivity. We begin to miss afforded opportunities to shift towards doing life together in full communion with each other [155] when we are closed off to seeing only a single way of prescribed life.

While my situation applies to an academic institution, this case could be applied to the church. Jennings urges the church to "follow our incarnate God into places, extending ourselves into the space and joining with the peoples..."[156] and letting go of patterns that naturalized division. As "others" are invited in from various life experiences, we must remember not to see, and judge them based on individual social identities and personal biases. They are homo sapiens, part of the human race created by God and are the sum of biological traits, experiences, intellect, emotional life, relationships, and geographical or national context.[157]

Similar to the people in Jane Elliot's exercise, who came willingly to be included in something that may have a greater

---

155 Jennings, *Acts*, 22
156 Jennings, *Acts*, 249
157 Bantum, *The Death Race*, 24

impact, although not fully understanding how that would happen, they did not come to be segregated or treated differently based on pressures associated with social identities. Instead, the church should be a safe environment where all people can be seen for whom they are while working to obtain what they came for.

There are many reasons people are drawn to a church, just as there are many reasons they "run" away. The challenge is realizing that for the many reasons they are drawn, the primary reason is God. Therefore, it is imperative that God is seen, felt, heard, and experienced from the moment one enters beyond the moment they leave.

We cry to God for freedom but still move and hold on to traditions that keep us enslaved rather than living freely with The Father. Where one should find a place of refuge, has also become, for some, a place of further oppression. How can we expect to be free, claim to desire to see freedom but the very place we hold on to oppressive traditions are in the very place people come for deliverance?

We have followed a religion that has become distorted and taken away the original foundation in which the church was built. We have followed traditions set by humans, who many refer to as the founders of our faith. We have failed to understand the gravity of their intents in formulating their doctrines. Perhaps, this is why lately we have seen God perform a major overhaul in many of our churches today. Many of our churches and leaders have developed rules to follow based upon our culture, rather than the culture of the original biblical writers and audience. Christianity and the ways of the church and her people have become deeply rooted in Eurocentric Culture. What we follow, especially in the US is a westernized religion, derailed from eastern traditions on which it was founded. We have become so enthralled with the history of the church dating back to Constantine, rather than understanding the significance of the time.

The era has become the foundation, or roots, as a man has become the leader of the people. All actions from this era have become the infrastructure of what many continue to follow. The foundations of the missions and establishment of churches are engrained in the historical content of actions dating back to Christianity in Rome rather than the lives of those who sacrificed to spread the gospel, as written on the pages of our sacred text. The foundations for conversion have become encrusted in Eurocentric roots. When the roots of the way began with God, he taught the people how to live according to his ways. Nothing was left uncovered. Instructions were provided for the home, marriage, raising children, living in community (outside the home), government, finances, banking (loans/borrowing), and so much more. While we can argue that times have changed, the basic principles of these lessons remain unchanged. These basic principles can be applied to every aspect of life, with the ultimate principle was to stay connected to and follow God's commands or instructions. Even as leaders rise throughout the generations it is important to keep these principles etched in our hearts. Doing so further confirms our godly relationship, therefore our weight of dependence on God and man does not become skewed.

I cannot negate that we have much to learn from the former leaders as their works, studies, and lives have enriched our lives. As much as we can learn what to do, we must also learn what not to do. It is important that we also understand the struggles they faced which became the basis upon which their dogma was established. This gives insight to the traditions we continue to follow today. We can come to understand how and why we understand issues such as salvation, which speaks even greater to the churches' divide on our practices. We should essentially see the same if we were following God versus man, thereby eliminating the discord amongst different practices of Christianity. Seeing the same does not imply we would all become clones. Rather what we should see is God and his decision to move in different ways in the lives of his people. Afterall, if there is discord amongst the church, or body of Christ, then how can we make a difference in the world? We are becoming the greater stumbling block and blindfold in the world seeing or connecting with God.

It is time to take the remove the blindfolds, boundaries, and barriers that limit our ability to see, connect and live with God.

The Light of Grace

In *The Cost of Discipleship*, Dietrich Bonhoeffer challenges the reader to explore how we view decisions of following Christ. As he describes the differences between cheap and costly grace, the reader begins to examine the context of our decision-making process and answering the call of discipleship. Furthermore, the author makes us take a hard look at what discipleship means to each individual and if our perspective aligns with biblical principles or if we have adjusted these principles to cling to our own presentation of the gospel because we somehow believe that following Christ is unbearable or impossible.

Bonhoeffer defines the concepts of cheap and costly grace, helping the reader to understand the value of obedient discipleship and the dangers of Christians living like the rest of the world. He implies that one of the greatest enemies of the church is cheap grace. He defines cheap grace as grace without discipleship. He uses the parable of the three men, yet I will highlight the lesson of the third man. The third man believes he can follow Christ under his own conditions rather the conditions of Christ. In this case, who is he really following? He is no longer following Christ. He is still submitted to and following himself. He has neither surrendered nor given up anything. He has failed to demonstrate neither faith nor obedience. This makes Christians no different than anyone else and having a significant impact on how others see or feel about faith.

In contrast, Bonhoeffer defines that costly grace compels us to submit to Christ. Under costly grace, he implies that a man would give up or sell what he has to follow Christ. This is what makes grace costly.[158] Bonhoeffer uses the example of Peter, who leaves his net to follow Christ. Peter's net is significant as he is a fisherman, and this tool is used to help him make a living. Peter lays this down in faith and obedience to follow Christ. It is important to note that Peter's response was not in part of a legalistic response in which he believed that if he gave up something to follow, he would receive something in return. Bonhoeffer stresses that discipleship and obedience should not be considered legalistic or deed based.

The theme of costly grace is emphasized throughout the section of Grace and Discipleship as Bonhoeffer attacks different areas or barriers that challenge us in following Christ. He implores us to examine our theology or doctrines we create, which can result in a watered-down gospel. Such messages deter us from making conscious and spontaneous decisions to answer the call of Christ as we justify our actions with our interpretations of the gospel. This results in eliminating the need for simple obedience. Also, as we are called, we fail to deny ourselves falling under the assumption that because Christ suffered then, we are not called to do the same. The road of the disciple comes without a cross to bear.

Furthermore, we are challenged to deal with individual accountability. So much emphasis is made about community and what Christ did for humanity as a whole, but Bonhoeffer challenges us to deal with our individual call to discipleship and what that may look like for the individual. He makes us explore what discipleship means to the individual and what one is willing to give up for it.

---

158 (Bonhoeffer 2001), 45

Obedience and Faith

Bonhoeffer states that there is no road to faith or discipleship, no other road – only obedience to the call of Jesus.[159] He implies that as we are called by Christ, we must understand that we are called to leave our old life behind and completely surrender. The way we surrender is through the spontaneous and obedient response to his call. He suggests that in the concept, of obedience, we are naturally challenged by what we believe. It is our belief that stifles us from obedience.

Bonhoeffer suggests that only the obedient believe which means we must obey a concrete demand.[160] He implies that as Christ calls, we are to make a conscious decision to respond to the call in the act of faith for faith and obedience cannot be separated. While some may believe this is a long process, Bonhoeffer implies that the decision is made somewhat in an instant.[161] For each moment one decides not to respond or delays their response, they are in fact still responding. For every moment we delay, we are consciously not stepping forward in the presupposition of faith and being obedient to the call of Christ. Once the decision is made to step forward, the real work now begins.

Bonhoeffer contributes our lack of spontaneous obedience to doubt and reflection. He implies that in the moments of reflecting upon our decision we contemplate relinquishing control of our lives. We are stuck between freedom and rationalizing the fundamentals of moral difficulties. I would agree that the misguided notion that once one steps out in obedience that they are now subjected to walk in a life of

---

159 (Bonhoeffer 2001), 58
160 (Bonhoeffer 2001), 64
161 (Bonhoeffer 2001), 73

perfection causes many to waiver in the space of cheap grace and disobedience. It is somehow tied to the same ability to misinterpret the Word of God.

Paradoxical Interpretation and Self Accountability

Another barrier we create in following Christ is what he calls paradoxical interpretation of Jesus' words. Bonhoeffer would suggest that our interpretations make it impossible to surrender our will to the call of Christ. Instead, we overuse or improperly use phrases like "God meets us where we are," thereby providing space for cheap grace. It is in this space that we are not forced to change or let go of our presuppositions or conditions. Instead, we use our rationalized theology to justify our actions or inability to take action. In his theology, Bonhoeffer does well in addressing this issue, which encourages us not to rebel against the call of God.

Bonhoeffer describes the idea of learning to suffer as a way of dealing with the "God meets us where we are" statement. He argues that in some way, we are all called to give up something or carry a particular cross, based on what we are called to bear. His ideas seem to imply that the call is not a one size fit all ordeal although "the cross is laid on every Christian."[162] This would imply that our experiences are or will be different based on where we are when called by Christ. This does not alleviate us from being obedient and surrendering ourselves to Christ. The problem, Bonhoeffer points out, is that we do not want to die. Not literally die but figuratively. We have an innate desire to stay comfortable. But what are we staying comfortable in? Bonhoeffer would suggest that we are staying comfortable enslaved to ourselves. He would suggest that taking on the suffering of following God is not

---

162 (Bonhoeffer 2001), 89

really suffering. In fact, he states, that to follow the way of the cross brings peace and refreshment to the soul and is the highest joy.[163]

I appreciate his use of the practical application to show how we try to reason with the word of God to justify our actions and how this causes a barrier in obediently following Christ. For instance, he points out how we understand that we are not to be anxious for nothing. Our way of rationalizing this scriptural reference is to focus on the idea that God understands we must work to provide for our families. Therefore, it is justifiable to be anxious.[164] In this type of situation, we may find ourselves outwardly tied to prosperity,[165] which is causing the anxiety, therefore, should one be compelled to follow God in a situation, they will have difficulty doing so.

A friend mentioned that as a minister, he finds himself struggling to take a stand on matters he knows are wrong because his position as a minister would be in jeopardy. This friend mentioned the anxiety of having to provide for their family. I believe this is an example of applying Bonhoeffer's theology. The decision for my friend is truly deciding on where to place his faith. Does he step out on faith and be obedient to what he believes is the way of Christ or rationalize his decision based on comfort or anxiety over a current position that he believes brings him prosperity? As one who has lost a job for standing on my beliefs, I would say the former is the way to go, though it is not an easy road to travel.

When I made my decision to take this stance, I was faced with questions of why, along with persuasions to change. In-

---

163 (Bonhoeffer 2001), 93
164 (Bonhoeffer 2001), 81
165 (Bonhoeffer 2001), 80

dividuals could not understand why I insisted that changing would not be the right thing even if my job security depended on it. They could not understand how or why I insisted on putting my livelihood on the line though I explained that what I was doing was my true job and I must see it until the end despite how painstaking it was.

My trust was placed in following Christ, and things worked out, not just for me but for those I stood up for. Some would think it did not work because I lost my job, but when the time came, I left in complete peace and was prepared for my departure. I would assume this is the peace Bonhoeffer speaks of when he refers to Christ's message in Matthew 11:29-30. There is peace for us in the yoke and burden of Christ.

Church Application

In reflecting on the contemporary relevance of this text, I thought of Bonhoeffer's idea that we should follow Christ with childlike obedience.[166] From a pastoral perspective, it is vital that we exemplify this childlike obedience in following Christ if we desire to make an impact in this world. Based on conversations I have had with people I would agree with Bonhoeffer that many believe that following Christ can feel like either a daunting task or that having the faith to follow as he calls is impossible. I would illustrate the idea of childlike obedience by comparing how children willingly follow their parents.

Here is my example. Not long ago, I was speaking to my son, who is now a young adult. He mentioned how he hated not having the foresight of plans that I included him in. He complained about how while he understood that growing up, my parents would drag us around never telling us where we

---

166 (Bonhoeffer 2001), 73

were going, and we followed without question, but for him, this did not work. He needed to know where we were going and what we were doing as this would keep down his anxiety.

I see my son's idea of following, much like how people struggle to follow Christ compared to how I see following Christ. While he sees that my parents dragged us around, I see that we followed our parents without question because we trusted them. We had no reason to question where we were heading, nor would we ever feel anxious about where we were heading. If anything, we rode looking out the window, enjoying the view and the time we spent together. There was something about our parents holding our hand that made us feel safe. We used the opportunity to listen to our parents talk, share wisdom, laugh, joke, have fun, and just take in whatever we could from the experience. Doing so, left no room for anxiety for we were preoccupied. Plus, we understood there was no reason for us to try to control any part of our lives at that moment. Our parents had everything in control. All we had to do was listen, follow, and be obedient. Things would work out, not only at the moment, but it helped us for the future as well.

This should be how we are following Christ. If we are following and focused on him, rather than ourselves or anything else around us, then it leaves less room for anxiety. The struggle is relinquishing control of our lives to the one that has been providing for us all along. Somehow, we believe that we have been and must continue to control every aspect of our life. Somehow we have grown to believe that we now understand or know better than the one who we are meant to follow. As Bonhoeffer states, through following Christ, we actually begin to transcend our comprehension by allowing ourselves to be led without knowing all.[167] This is the same way Abraham was led. He had no idea where he was going, yet he got up and went, allowing God to lead him. Abraham lost family members and friends along the way, yet he still followed.

While this is an Old Testament story, it is still a relevant example of childlike obedience in spontaneously responding to the call of God. It is through Abraham's example we can witness Bonhoeffer's definition of the costly grace of discipleship. By examining his story and thinking of how we follow our parents, we can examine how we have responded to the call of Christ compared to the challenging theology of Dietrich Bonhoeffer. Then we must ask ourselves, are we part of the problem of cheapening grace or doing our part to fight for costly grace?

---

167 (Bonhoeffer 2001), 93

Starting Over

In Exodus 32:7-14, we witness an aspect of God and Moses' relationship in an intimate conversation as Moses pleads for the people, and God moves.

In Genesis 18:18-33, we witness an aspect of The Lord's and Abraham's relationship in an intimate conversation as Abraham pleads for the people of Sodom, and the Lord moves.

In Genesis 3:8, even when Adam and Eve sinned in the garden, they heard the sound of the Lord God walking in the garden. How? Because they had a relationship with Him. They knew Him, not just of Him.

As we begin to study the early life of Christ, we can see that even as a young boy, He knew God, His Father. When Mary and Joseph found Jesus in the temple, they did not understand what He was doing there and why he has caused them such anxiety and stress as they searched for him. Jesus replied to them, "Why did you seek Me? Did you not know that I must be about My Father's business? (Luke 2:49, New King James Version) Such maturity and wisdom he displayed understanding (not just knowing) that nothing He did nor would do was ever about Him.

Later, in John 2, we read the first recorded miracle Jesus performed, turning water into wine during a wedding in Cana. It is interesting that this miracle is spoken about more than most other miracles, often too because it is the subject of alcohol debates. What we overlook are very key aspects of understanding relationships.

Mary comes to Jesus and to tell him the wine is out. Understanding that carrying on traditional or cultural norms to fulfill personal wishes and desires was not the essence of his ministry, He responds, "what does this have to do with me?" Understanding that this celebration has nothing to do with the timing of what He was sent to do, He reiterates, "My hour has not yet come." It is the relationship between a son and mother that moves Jesus to honor this request of his mother, but it is for us to witness and understand this had nothing to do with why God sent Him. Perhaps this is also why we oversimplify this particular miracle and make it so "commonly" spoken of. This act is permitted by God as we see an important relationship between mother and son, but more importantly, Honor to His Father and honoring why His Father sent Him. Again, we witness the true essence of relationships.

Throughout His ministry, Jesus would continuously refer to His Father regarding His work and His purpose. If he wasn't speaking about it, He still demonstrated it. Honoring the Deuteronomic laws which prohibited anyone from worshiping man, Jesus, as He walked in the flesh. He was careful to not have those that followed worship Him but to see God in everything He said and did.

Why was this important? Because as He would continue to demonstrate how to live with God here on earth, how to live in covenant with God, live in a relationship with God, work according to the expectation of God, and He wanted us to see how to carry on after He ascended. We were to follow in the steps of Christ, work to live as Christ did, follow spiritual disciplines that would align ourselves with God and His Word.

In doing so, we reconnect forming genuine relationships with The Father, carrying the essence of Christ (The Holy Spirit). We become embodied once again and not in these broken relationships, we see established that have people running in the opposite direction of God.

In The Spirit of The Disciplines, by Dallas Willard, he contends that the secret of entering into an easy yoke is to embody the life of Christ. The analogy he gives of a child's desire to emulate a ballplayer[168] is profound. The idea that one would desire to be so much like a star athlete that it may appear the necessary things needed are to adorn similar gear. Unfortunately, the true test comes at performance time, and they are not equipped to handle a given situation.

It is interesting that he uses the analogy of a child parallel to emulating the life of Christ. Adults would quickly teach a child the reality of discipline versus emulation. As Willard points out, we could apply the same application of disciplines to our faith. Willard implies that we would much rather avoid the pains of discipline and therefore, miss out on the easy yoke[169] or make it easy for ourselves in the long run.

Nothing can replace a life of preparation and dedication, even if that life comes with pains. The preparation of life may seem burdensome as one must be committed and make sacrifices. But, when it is time to perform, it comes easily and naturally, without thought and hesitation, like muscle memory. Following the Life of Christ should be a natural embodiment of who we are and how we live. The way of life becomes a natural pattern or design of who we are and how to carry ourselves. Whatever comes up in life, we are not stopping to

---

168 (Willard 1991), 3
169 (Willard 1991), 7

contemplate how to respond because it is a natural part of who we are.[170]

This is the foundation of relationship!! It is time to check and reset our relationship with God.

Dallas Willard's view of Dualism, in essence, sees that human life is not what it should be. The implication is that we can live at a higher level than we currently are or believe we can. This theory is also at the art of transcending as it relates to Christian Discipleship.

Willard believes that since our bodies were twisted out of proper shape and proportion due to the fall caused by sin, we have the capability to rise and reform.[171]

He implies we have a body to have at our disposal and the resources that would allow us to be persons in fellowship and cooperation with a personal God.[172] We have a part in our body's transformation. Unfortunately, spiritually we are starving, therefore too weak to transcend[173] because weakness causes out bodies to yield to (other) influences.[174]

The life of Christian discipleship allows us to reconnect thereby to live again with and (unto) God. His Cornstalk analogy[175] exemplifies the human capability of transcending, whereas discipleship is like water to a cornstalk, transcending the plant inwardly and then extending it outwardly. Our discipleship changes us inwardly, resurrect-

---

170 (Willard 1991), 9
171 (Willard 1991), 63
172 (Willard 1991), 92
173 (Willard 1991), 63
174 (Willard 1991), 92
175 (Willard 1991), 65

ing us outwardly to our (original) positions and connecting us with God.

To be in relationship with God, our mind and body must come under subjection. It is commonly accepted that our thoughts influence our actions and we are thus called to "be transformed by the renewing of our minds" thereby changing what and how we think. We must engage in spiritual disciplines that help transform our thoughts through the formation of new habits. Spiritual disciplines transform us by strengthening our spirits and allowing us to connect with God, and they ultimately help us flourish as human beings. How can we claim to know God without the intimacy needed, which comes through our physical, spiritual disciplines? This would substantiate the argument that causes division on things like how and when God speaks and moves in a person's life. Through this intimacy, we begin to have greater or deeper experiences with God, coming into contact with Him beyond what our natural minds would otherwise comprehend.

Part II

FINDING FAITH IN GOD

Faith To See

How can we say we believe in God yet only have faith in things that make sense to us, things we can comprehend, or be certain of? God calls us to have faith and to trust in The Lord with all of our heart and lean not on our own understanding, yet our understanding is the one thing we trust to lean on; therefore, believing it is the absolute thing that holds us up.

We read the bible and tell the stories of the old and new testament, but are they just stories to us? Have we become so accustomed to "preaching" and teaching what is written only to give some practical life lesson or word of encouragement to get us and others through the week? Have we watered down what is written to only passing down "stories" forgetting about the demonstration and application of what lies within The Word?

What has become of believers today? Have we sub come to being addicts? Requiring a weekly message of so-called hope or encouragement that will get us week to week with nothing ever taking us beyond the feeding tubes of the preacher's pulpit? What happened to actual demonstration of faith and trust?

Perhaps, there is no faith because there is no demonstration. Maybe there is no demonstration because there is no faith. We have put our faith and trust in the wrong hands.

We believe what man says over what God says. We believe man has the final word. If a man says you shall die, then we believe death is inevitable. If man says there is only one cure, then that is what we believe. If man says, God can only heal a certain way, then that is what we believe. Since when does man determine the parameters in which God can and will work?

Last I checked, He was God. Last I checked, He was the Creator...man did not create God. God created man.

How did we get here? How has man placed himself in the position of a god, therefore, making all the decisions and determinations and having the final say? How did we get here? Where man believes man over God? Where man frowns at the possibility of God doing the impossible, unimaginable, and unthinkable?

How did we get here? Where we argue over man determining the value of a life that was given as a gift from God? How did we get here? Where a person's beliefs in God becomes questioned as 'ethical" or "sane" simply because someone does not agree?

How did we get here? Where a person's sanity becomes questioned because they have the faith to follow God?

Just because you do not understand or because you cannot comprehend the magnitude of someone's beliefs does not mean you get to change their narrative to meet your level of understanding.

Harriett Tubman has been affectionately called the Black Moses. She was known to have visions, out-of-body experiences, and spoke of hearing God. It is interesting that you can find different narratives of her story, depending on the beliefs of the storyteller. Those who may not fully comprehend or have doubts about God and/or experiencing God's the supernatural will diminish her experiences and attribute them to head injuries she sustained early in life. This is not to negate the fact she sustained those injuries. The point is, Mrs. Tubman, explicitly described her experiences. She contributed these experiences to the great work she accomplished helping to free slaves through the underground railroad.

Why is it important to change the narrative to the story?

Because as much as we study the Bible, reading about God speaking to and guiding people, somehow, we cannot believe God still speaks. Sure, we say he does, but we don't actually believe it. If we did, we would not cling to every word out the mouth or every man as much as we do. We would have greater faith than we do. We would actually learn from what we read in the Bible rather than repeating the lessons over and over. We would stop chalking medical miracles up to anomalies and praise God for the work He does. We would praise God in life and at the end of suffering (death). We would live greater and fuller lives with God. We would have greater faith...greater trust...greater belief. We would see greater demonstration because we took God out of the box and realized that faith is not a hyperbole.

Faith To Overcome

I sat one morning at 6 am in tears, praying and crying to my Father to fight for what He has promised me, for I admit that over the days prior, I had been tired and weak.

I had been under what seemed like constant increasing spiritual. I also found out that what I knew to be true was confirmed. Many members of my family have been behind a lot of the spiritual backlash I have been receiving. Those who preach the Word of God, who would teach to not put your mouth on God's anointed, had actually done just that and in great numbers, as they gather together to slander and curse me while elevating themselves. Meanwhile stating, I want to pray for you or I need to "cover you," which was something I never accepted, as I knew their words were not coming from a righteous place.

At one point, I tried telling someone how I felt about everything, which was received with an "I understand" response. With the quick in turn response, I knew they truly did not, for they too had been part of the long-standing problem. The problem of hypocrisy, slander, false loyalty, and never really helping to intervene instead only the cause of iniquity and bloodshed. This despite the years of faithfulness on my part. The committal of prayers, mentorship, leadership, love, and support in more ways than one can imagine that came in the sheer sacrifice that has been underappreciated, dismissed and overlooked because my "platform" is not big enough.

Nonetheless, I prayed for my Father to step in where others have failed. I needed Him to take over. I needed Him to break loose these chains of oppression and injustice. To break the curses spoken over the life of my son and me so that we may continue to move forward in clarity towards the promises Yahweh has spoken, for we are so close yet now things seemed so far away. This was not a time for Him to forsake us, rather to WAR on our behalf. For I would not lay down and "die" though tired and I would use whatever breath I had left in my body to cry out for ADONAI to SAVE us. To rain down and cast out every darkness hovering over us. For it was indeed time to repay the enemy for all he has done! It was time for the redeemer to rise among us.

I sat in prayer as I heard Him tell and guide me to change the worship music I listened to. I put on ANWA Worship at the Well 2. "Flow 'Oh How We Need You'" was playing in the background as I cried out. Then as I sat in silence, waiting on a response, to hear Him speak. The end of the song began to play, which begins to sound like a battle cry. I heard Him say, when the enemy comes in like a flood, the Lord raises up a standard against him. So, I went to the Word and pulled up Isaiah 59:19 and began reading all of Isaiah 59.

Now, as I got towards the end and began to feel reassured, then inspired to write, I open Microsoft Word. I began to type, and the song changes to "Hallelujah." Listen, you need to understand that this is not the next song on the track on the playlist. This is the first song on the album. "Oh, How We Need You," was the fifth track. I knew, that was God confirming His message to me early that morning. No one can ever tell me anything different. I know everything will be ok. I know he will fight for me. I know he has heard me. The enemy has been put on notice, and we are moving forward! The album continued to play as normal afterward!

I share this as many wonder if and how God will ever answer us. The challenge is that we too easily dismiss things as a coincidence or happenstance, but we took time to understand who God is and who He is in our lives, perhaps we can stop dismissing Him when He speaks or answers us in various ways that meet our needs. God does answer, we just have to be open to hear, listen, and acknowledge.

Faith to Trust

Peace I leave you; my peace I give you. I do not give to you as the world gives. Do not let your hearts be troubled and do not be afraid. (John 14:27)

Have I not commanded you? Be strong and courageous. Do not be afraid; do not be discouraged, for the Lord, your God will be with you wherever you go. (Joshua 1:9)

So many have been commanded by God to do something they never imaged doing and to accomplish what so many thought was the impossible task. But as The Father sent each one forth, He continuously reminded them that no matter what, he would be with them along the way. Too often, we sit on dreams, goals, and plans because we are fearful. We are afraid of what others may think and feel. Afraid of how we may be perceived. Afraid of failing. Afraid that if we just take a chance, nothing will work out. We get trapped in the inevitable circle of "what if..." While it is ok, to question the plans, goals, and dreams to ensure they are righteous or to ensure we are following the path God has laid before us and not something we are doing on our own, without wisdom and purpose, it is NOT ok to stay in a constant state of "question" or "confusion."

It is important to understand that just as The Father gives us direction, He provides the provision to accomplish what He desires of us. Everything we need to continue to move ahead is available for the taking if we keep our sights on Him. It is when we turn our head, our heart, and our mind away, that we become lost and confused. This is when fear takes over and lead us astray. This is when we end up moving in a direction that was never designed for us. We allow fear to drive us down the road of destruction and failure.

Staying obedient and faithful to the call will lead us to destiny, the place designed for us. As we stay faithful and walking in faith, The Lord, His grace, His power, His Love, and His strength, will cause you to prevail. With Him, we are able to accomplish what people believe is impossible, unattainable, and inconceivable. The difference between the faithful and the fearful is who and what we put our trust in.

The fearful have difficulty moving forward because their minds keep them hostage. The fearful are unable to see beyond what is presently in front of them. They hold on to the thoughts and beliefs of people and things around them. They put their trust in systems and organizations, first, looking at what others accomplished through various sources, trials, and errors. These ways create nothing but barriers or hindrances that ultimately cause us to become trapped. Trapped in the snare of inevitable failure. Trapped and weak, shut up and shut off from what should be giving your dreams, goals, and plans life. Those plans, goals, and dreams, eventually just die, leaving the fearful in darkness and further despair, believing there is no hope and no future.

The faithful, on the other hand, trust in another source. They understand that the true meaning of faith is the ability to "believe" in something greater than themselves. The Word tells us that faith is the substance of things hoped for, the evidence of things not seen (Hebrews 1:1). They understand that though they cannot see it now, the mere fact that these dreams, goals, and plans, were planted in their heart by The One that created them, this is what they can trust. They understand that it was not without reason or purpose that God spoke, telling the results, first, and that is more than enough to move forward. Think about that for a moment...He gave the results to us before we stepped forward. He basically gave you a reason to get and move.

Through His words, telling you what He would do, as the outcome, He was already telling you that the way straight, was the path He created for you to arrive at your destination. The plan was created before you accepted it. Everything is set before you, and the only thing required of you is to move. That's it...move. He is The Creator. He knows the end from the beginning. He goes before us. Therefore, we can rest assure that there is nothing to fear. He knows what we will encounter along the way (seen and unseen), and He will equip us with whatever we need as we complete our work for His purpose. When trials come, he strengths us to persevere. Even as neigh Sayers, the unbelievers, the doubters, and the skeptics come to discourage and persuade you to turn off your path...to lose your footing...God is still there, keeping you encouraged. Reminding you of His presence. Most of all, when needed, when we become weak and downtrodden, He will pick us up and carry us along the way.

See, the fearful will never understand how all of this can happen simply because they are stuck in a pattern of belief that limits them. Meanwhile, the faithful understand that we rely on a source that is unlimited in His ways, His thinking, and actions. We rely on the source that is beyond our comprehension, therefore understanding that anything is possible as long as we believe and put all our trust in Him.

When we say, "God, I trust you," we should mean just that. This should not be a conditional thing or phrase. We cannot trust God only when times are good, and things are going our way. Trust is believing in God all the time. Trust is not believing what God can provide, it comes from knowing and understanding who He is.

See, we like to trust God for things. Unfortunately, this comes with a false understanding of what our relationship with Him should be like. God is not just a giver of things we celebrate and praise only after receiving something. He is our help and sustainer. God is always there, watching and listening to us. He knows when we are tired and weak. He knows our needs well before we go before Him crying in despair. By the time we have gone to Him, He has already set things in motion to provide for us. When we really, really trust and believe in God, we can keep our heads lifted up in times of trouble. We do not have to go about "making a way" or "try to figure things out." It is during those times when we should truly be using the words, "God I Trust you." This is when we show that we believe in the one from where our help comes from.

It is easy to believe and trust when we see things happen, but when the going gets tough...well, these are the times when He wants us to hold true to our words. One thing, I have learned over the years, is that God seems to hold us very accountable to our words. As soon as we go about telling everyone how great He is and all that He has done for us, it seems those are the times "the bottom falls out." I have been there time and time again. I call it the "Job Season."

Have you ever really paid attention to the beginning of Job? He was such a faithful servant, strong in his belief. Then one day, the adversary tries to tell God that Job only believes and trusts God because God has protected him. The adversary believes that if God did not have a fence around Job, then Job would basically no longer trust and believe in God. This is much like our daily narratives. As long as we feel protected, we trust, but what happens when we are tried by the adversary? What happens when he comes and rocks our world trying to take everything away? What happens when he seems to destroy everything, we worked so hard to maintain or achieve? What happens when things get dark and gray, and there seems to be no way out? Will we still say, "God, I Trust you?"

It is hard. This I know for certain. Yet, I want to encourage you that these are the times when we must trust and believe the most. These are times when we must activate our Faith, not in what God can do, but simply in who He is.

When we trust God, especially in times of trouble, we are saying, "I have no idea how things are going to turn around, but I believe that because He is God, I will make it through." "I have no idea what the road ahead will look like, but if He says go, I will trust that He will see me through this."

We must learn to trust God when He says Go, stay, move, or even when He says, "No, not yet." Whoa, what? God says, "No?" Well, isn't that hard to believe? But yes, we have to trust even when He says, "No." Remember, He knows what we need even before we realize it. So, that also means that when we believe something may be right for us, He will say, "No." Why? because for those things, we are attempting or trying to attain, He is letting us know that this is not what He had in mind, these are the things we have tried to makeshift to provide for ourselves.

We have to trust that when He stops us in our tracks of piecing our lives together, that He has our best interest in His heart and mind. He knows more than what we see. Therefore, he knows the turn of events that will come when we are thinking about heading in a certain direction. As our Help, He is helping us stay away from what will cause us trouble.

God our help, keeps us from trouble and restless nights. He protects us from situations that will cause us harm and despair. But when we start leaning on our own understanding, trying to "figure things out," well trouble and despair is inevitable. Why? Because we did not trust Him. We thought we now had to become our provider. We thought it was time to take control of our lives, walking away from what God has set up for us. Then we want to blame God. Well, the truth is we are the ones to blame. We just said we trusted Him, but when we couldn't figure out the next move...when we could not see the light ahead, when we did not understand how things would work, then we stop believing. We take our eyes off God and begin looking, searching, and creating a means for ourselves.

It is like when we have an item to put together, and it came with instructions. We are so excited to put this together, but because the instructions seem so complex or lengthy, we glance them over and then toss them aside. We begin our project, believing we can do this without the very instructions that came with the item. Sometimes, we make it work. We get the item together and perhaps took a few short cuts. "Oh yeah!" We got it together. It is all in one piece, and we feel proud as we stick out our chest in what we have accomplished. But how long will that last? How sturdy it is? Oh, and just how many pieces did we have "leftover" because we left them out?

This is like our lives. We skip steps and leave important pieces out when we take our eyes off God and start "figuring things out" on our own. Yes, things look good for the moment, but exactly how long will this last? We created a temporary fix when God provides a permanent path of safety for us. I do not know about you, but to keep having temporary fixes seems like an awful lot more work. It may be tough to stick out the process, but at least I know I will not be back around this way again, doing the same thing in the near future. I would much rather keep moving forward, trusting God, than moving in constant circles wearing myself out. I am just not about that life.

So, I ask, if you really trust God? Have you been really trusting God, or have you been in a state of trust based only on what you see? It is time to evaluate what we are saying and believing and take it up a notch. Let's move forward, trusting who God is and not just what He has done for us. God is our keeper, he will never fore sake you nor leave you. Trust in Him and sing those praises of trust even when we cannot see the road ahead. Know that, no matter what comes our way, He is there with us, providing our every need, even before we knew the need existed.

Thankfully, God gave me an example to follow in learning what it means to trust God. He gave me Uncle E. As a child, I wanted so badly to learn more about God, perhaps, more than what most people were aware of. I would run behind cousins, who went to church just so I could go with them. I remember sitting in a "youth group" and watching Uncle E teach these young people. He stood tall and confident and just had a way of communicating with these young people that I admired. You know, sometimes, the older generation could have a way of talking to/teaching the younger generation that does not always come off well. Sometimes, even when they may not intend to, they can be a little...well, belittling. Not Uncle E, he connected with these young people and captivated their attention.

Periodically, over the years, I would find myself in conversations with Uncle E, and these conversations would leave me with lifelong lessons. Once, as I was going through a tough time and had a lot of questions, it was Uncle E that introduced me to the Book of Job. It was one of his favorites and later would become one of mine, as well. I admit, at first, I did not get it. Like many, all I could think was, "Man, Job went through so much!" "Why did he have to endure so much?"

Job, a faithful servant, seemed to have lost everything and everyone around him. People seemed to turn on Job as they did not understand how he stayed so faithful and trusting of a God that made him suffer. Some tried to give reasons why he suffered the way he did as if Job did something wrong. There were times, in which Job even cried out to God, trying to make sense of it all. Yet, in everything Job declares, "Though He slay me, yet will I trust Him; but I will maintain mine own ways before Him" (Job 13:15 KJV). This is undeniable faith to trust in God, no matter what it looks like.

I have watched (even from a distance) my uncle battle challenges that most could or would not comprehend. In everything he has faced and continues to face, the one thing that has not changed is his example of Trusting God. When it seems like all hope is lost or when some just do not understand, he has trusted God, just as Job did. See, it is one thing to read about stories of Trust amid trials, yet it is another to witness it in real life. These real-life examples are those that stick with you the most. These examples allow you to see the God you read about, and these examples are sometimes, what we need to strengthen our own walk/relationship with God.

As an adult, I, too, have been faced with my own trials. Sometimes, it has felt like I have lost everything and everyone. Sometimes, it appears that no one really understands but one thing is for sure, in everything, I continue to trust God. When things fall apart, or it seems there is no hope, I still trust God. When others come like "friends of Job" to suggest a plan B or to quit, I say, "No, I will trust God." Even when I do not understand, I trust God. Is this not what God wants of us, to just trust Him? Not just trust Him when life is full of sunshine and roses but to do so when the clouds are gray?

We say that we trust God with all of our heart and soul, but when the road gets tough, how often are you ready to bail? Ready to figure out your own plan? Ready to go your separate way and curse God? For me, no matter how many times, I get knocked down or the road gets too tough to bear, I will trust God. No one or nothing can change that because when some gave up hope, and I carried on, He always brought me through and greater than I ever expected.

I cannot say I would have never learned to trust God by just reading Job. I can say that despite all my uncle has endured, I am grateful that by watching him, He has taught me what it truly means to Trust God, a life lesson I will never forget. It is interesting that watching him teach, when I was young and how he continued to encounter young people, I too would later grow to do the same. Little did he know that long ago there was an impartation that would stick with me many years later. Before I would get there, I had to endure my own journey, holding on to the spoken and demonstrated lessons he taught me.

God has given me a heart for the younger generation, the next generation of leaders. Teaching them, helping them to grow, and leading them to become who God has called them to be for the generations still to come. Connections are important. God places people in our lives for reasons, but we often do not take the time to reflect on our connections. What are we learning from those God has connected us with? What does He want us to see and learn from them? Thanks to Uncle E, I learned to Trust God and the importance of connecting with a younger generation to lead them. Job is still one of my favorites, but now I read it with a different perspective.

Do you have an example of someone who demonstrated what it means to trust God?

Faith To Believe

Everything is possible for them that believe

Believe

Believe in what exactly?

Believe that with prayer anything is possible?
Believe that with action anything is possible?
Believe that with hope and faith, anything is possible?

Well, yes!

See, you need all three. Neither works without the other.

Too often we want to rely on one and forget about the other two. We believe that we can just have faith. Well, faith in what? Faith in who? First, you need to understand who you have faith in, which causes an action. That action is to gain understanding.

Understand who God is, for yourself, and understand how He is working in your life and what He expects of you. Ok, now that means you may have just hit another action. See, once you begin to understand this expectation, then you must begin to align yourself with such. What does he want you to do, how does he want you to do it, when does he want you do it, etc?

Guess what, there is your prayer. Yes, it can be that simple, but here is the second challenge, believing in prayer.

Believing that when you seek The Lord posing questions. He will answer. Whether those answers come directly or indirectly as he sends us answers and messages in so many ways, yet we must be open to receiving them.

He may use a conversation you may have with a friend or family member, a mentor, a song, or a TV program; you just never know, but one thing is for certain he always confirms his word, and it will align with the truth of the biblical scriptures.

If your heart is waxed cold and you refused to hear and believe then you will never receive what you seek. You are equivalent to a blind man, having no vision. But to those who believe and receive, you come back to the beginning of the cycle again. You are required to take action.

Yes, even after you have faith, and prayed, you still need action. God will give you a plan, he will give you the wisdom to implement such plans, but what good is it all if you put nothing into action? You cannot expect God to live your life for you. He gives us everything we need to live a fruitful and prosperous life. Unfortunately, too often we are "waiting" on God to move, wondering why nothing is working out, yet we have all the faith in the world. Well, I have news for you. God is waiting for you to move.

Too often we are simply waiting for God to show up and do something in our lives, but just as we are waiting on Him, He is waiting on us. He is waiting for us to come from our mundane life and take a leap of faith and realize that He already dwells among us. We need to open our eyes to see that He is here…there with you and in so many ways. As you encounter others, you may experience God's love. As you take in what is around you, you will witness his presence.

You don't have to go far to see or witness the power of God. You just have to open your eyes to the infinite ways he is near and present and believe.

The challenge with believing is that sometimes we pray and ask God to do certain things in our lives, we want or expect Him to do it the way we think. We expect what we are asking for to come in a way our natural minds would normally comprehend, but that is not how God will always work or show up. Because we are expecting things to be done a certain way, we could very well be rejecting the gift or answer to our prayers without even realizing it. We must learn to expect the unexpected things of God. Remember, whenever Christ healed the sick, He healed them where they were. Could he do it for you too? Possibly, it depends on your faith.

The greater the expectation, the greater the reward. If you set your sight, your mind, your faith on small expectations, then that shall be what you receive. That will be the outcome. We are to speak those things as if they were. Meaning to speak a thing into existence. Therefore, whatever you believe, you shall have. If your faith is small if you do not believe that God can do the impossible, the incredible, the unimaginable, that you shall not see it.

Those things can happen right before your very eyes, yet because you lack the faith to see it, you will remain blind to what exists.

We must keep in mind that the only thing keeping us from obtaining the promises of God is our lack of faith. Our inability to expect greater, therefore the inability to see and receive greater. In the flesh, we have created a system of time and existence that does not work according to the time and existence of God. We set limits, parameters, barriers, and guidelines that God does not work within.

Trust and believe that when he has placed something in your heart, He has set provisions for those things to flourish and well beyond what your mind may comprehend at the moment. The key is trusting and believing in Him to get you from the starting line to the finish line.

Remember, God, told Abram, "Go from your country and your kindred and your father's house to the land that I will show you. I will make of you a great nation, and I will bless you, and make your name great so that you will be a blessing. I will bless those who bless you, and the one who curses you I will curse: and in you, all the families of the earth shall be blessed" (Genesis 12:1-3). When Abram heard this, he went as the Lord instructed. He had no idea where he was going, but he trusted the Lord and His plans for him. He had no idea how God would do what he promised yet, he gathered his things, which apparently started with his faith, then headed forward. God blessed Abram (Abraham) and his barren wife Sara, with a son, which was considered the impossible, even to them. Their story continued well beyond what their mind would have ever comprehended, including the birth, death, and resurrection and continued testament of the life and power of Christ.

I get it. We can all struggle in our faith, but we must come to realize that even if we start small, we cannot stay there forever. If at first, you step out on a little faith, then you should continually increase or elevate your level of faith. How can you stay stuck in a place of small and mediocre when God has proven to you time and time again that He is there, listening, protecting, loving you, and providing for you? How can you believe God to be a great and mighty God yet expect him to move in only minute ways?

In Seminary, a group of us students were tasked with a close examination of Vigne Guroian's study of "The Case of Baby Rena," an 18-month-old patient who was dying of AIDS and heart disease. Her pain was so great that she required constant sedation. When simple procedures were performed on her, tears fell from her eyes, but the respirator tube prevented her from crying aloud. Guroian challenges us with the question, is the removal of life support killing Rena or allowing her to die with dignity? As we investigate the ethics of this case, we will call upon the articles "The Catholic Tradition on Forgoing Life Support" by Kevin D. O'Rourke and "Having Enough Faith Not to Be Healed" by John D. Brunt in *On Moral Medicine*.

Killing Baby Rena

Rena's foster parents espouse a deep Christian belief in the sanctity of life. The challenge here seems greater than accepting the death of a loved-one rather understanding and respecting the foster parent's belief of "spiritual sense of obedience to God" (Lysaught, 1109). The legal guardians believed that God told them to "take the child and rear her in the nurture and admonition of God's word...and to battle the spirits of infirmity."[176] The guardians were strongly supported by their community of friends and pastors in determining the way in which Rena lived and died. The family members or legal proxy are called upon to make decisions for the patients. They believe that "human life is considered a gift from the creator and the control of human life implies stewardship, not absolute autonomy."[177] Moving to palliative care, for the

---

176 (Lysaught, Kotva Jr and al. 2012), 1108
177 (Lysaught, Kotva Jr and al. 2012), 119

parents, was a way of allowing Rena to die and was contrary to what they believed was their role in her life. They believed they were sent by God to foster this child and fight infirmity.[178] Stopping treatment would mean they stopped fighting.

While many may look at prolonging life as a poor investment of energy, time, or money, these factors are not considered in the same aspect when one sees themselves as being stewards of human life.[179] Prolonging life is always the viable option and never considered a burden.[180] Drug therapy for patients with AIDS may offer hope of benefit, but some patients might deem it an excessive burden because of the expense involved.[181] Believing they were entrusted to fight for her life, medical intervention is beneficial for the patient[182] as it offers hope of benefit over excessive burden.[183]

Who is responsible for these decisions? The physician should present an opinion as to whether the means in question will cure, help significantly, or have no effect on the ailing patient's diagnosis and prognosis. Only the patient or proxy can determine factors of spiritual condition accurately. The source of this personal responsibility is the 'sacred and inviolable' character of the human person and not bioethics. Hence, the radical right to make the ethical decision concerning means to prolong life belongs to the patient.[184] The teachings of the Catholic Church to issues involving Catholic hospitals and nursing homes in the Ethical and Religious Directives, ERD,

---

[178] (Lysaught, Kotva Jr and al. 2012), 1109
[179] (Lysaught, Kotva Jr and al. 2012), 1119
[180] (Lysaught, Kotva Jr and al. 2012), 1118
[181] (Lysaught, Kotva Jr and al. 2012), 1123
[182] (Lysaught, Kotva Jr and al. 2012), 1120
[183] (Lysaught, Kotva Jr and al. 2012), 1123
[184] (Lysaught, Kotva Jr and al. 2012), 1125

implies that family concerns should be recognized when decisions about life support are being made by a patient.[185] Pius XII states that a family is bound only to use ordinary means to prolong life. Therefore, it implied that it still their choice to use to extraordinary means as well. This does not imply the family does not understand euthanasia, nor they are refusing to allow a relative to die based on natural humanistic reasons. Quite the opposite. It implies the family is entitled to their beliefs even if health professionals do not agree. The role of the health professional is to continue to educate without infringing on the spiritual beliefs of the patients, proxy, or their community. If this community has hope and faith in medicine, then the same respect should be given to their hope and trust in further spiritual beliefs.

In his essay *Having Enough Faith Not to Be Healed*, John Brunt asserts that if Christians are the true believers in Christ they purport to be, then accepting the "inevitability" of death under certain circumstances is one of the greatest acts of faith they can accomplish. According to Brunt, the Bible is clear that death is the "enemy" brought on by the fall of humanity. However, Jesus's death, burial, and resurrection rendered death the "defeated enemy"[186] and, therefore, Christians no longer need to fear the physical death of this world.

Jesus's sacrifice wholly eliminated the *spiritual* death of His followers (Revelation 2:11), Christians should not take this as a license to disregard the intrinsic value of earthly life and make flippant decisions of when it is no longer worth guarding. In the case of Baby Rena's treatment, we must ask, 'To who does the decision belong of when life is no longer worth

---

185 (Lysaught, Kotva Jr and al. 2012), 1126
186 (Lysaught, Kotva Jr and al. 2012), 1128

living?' For Rena's physicians, the choice was a professional one belonging to the attending staff. But for the girl's foster parents, her life was in the hands of their God to do with as He saw fit.

An Intrusion into Baby Rena's Death

Based on Baby Rena's diagnosis and prognosis the order to start comfort care measures by the physician is in the best interest of the patient because there are no procedures left in modern medicines bag of tricks. Modern medicine has hit its limits in this unfortunate case. The decision to withdraw Baby Rena from life support is not euthanasia. Comfort care orders are a plan of care when all possible medical endeavors have been exhausted, and the patient's condition has been deemed to be futile. This little girl is suffering tremendously. What some are calling treatment, Baby Rena is probably calling torture.

In his article, Guroian calls on the expertise of Daniel Callahan. Callahan makes it clear that there needs to be a distinction between euthanasia and palliative care. Callahan writes,

'Letting Die' is only possible if there is some underlying disease that will serve as the cause of death. Put me on a respirator now, when I am in good health, and nothing whatever will happen if it is turned off... Killing, by contrast, provides its own fatal pathology. Nothing but the action of the doctor giving the lethal injection is necessary to bring about death.'[187]

> When the patient comes off life support, no one knows how much time she has left, but they do know that her suffering will be minimized. There is a clear distinc-

---

187 (Lysaught, Kotva Jr and al. 2012), 1112

tion between actively taking a life and not giving them the treatment that will add to the despair.

Religion and spirituality is a valuable part of these decisions. Sometimes a family member's faith can be used to argue against sound medical information that would prevent unnecessary suffering. When faith is healthy and practiced in community that supports that patient's needs, rather than the personal interest of the family members, the inclusion of spiritual beliefs remains life-affirming, even in the decision to let go.

In the article "Having Enough Faith not to be Healed," John D. Brunt presents a perspective on faith and dying, which is important for our understanding of death and medical ethics. Brunt contends that while the Bible refers to death as the enemy, the Bible also asserts that death is a defeated enemy.[188] Brunt relies on the Bible's characterization of true faith to build his concept of how we ought to have faith. In the story of Shadrach, Meshach, and Abednego, all three assert that God can save them, and they pray that he will, but they continue to believe 'even if' he does not. This 'even if' is present in other biblical stories as well. Brunt asserts that we may pray for healing, but we must continue to have faith, even if healing does not occur.

In palliative care, patients receive comfort measures instead of curing measures. While some would argue that no longer trying to cure a patient demonstrates a lack of faith, Brunt argues that this demonstrates a deeper faith. This is faith in the value of the embodied person to be cared for in a meaningful way and faith in the resurrection, that this life is not all we have. Further, the move to palliative care demon-

---

188 (Lysaught, Kotva Jr and al. 2012), 1128

strates faith in God's larger plan, which may not be what feels best for us in the moment. Brunt argues that to suggest that a lack of faith is equivalent to a lack of healing is a form of shallow faith that is cruel.[189] Many people of deep faith are not healed and to blame them or their loved ones for lacking faith is hurtful. Instead, while we may hope and pray for a miracle, deep faith chooses to move forward 'even if' prayers are not answered as we might wish and to maintain that deep faith amid the pain.

The case ended in court with the family fighting not just to continue their choice of treatment, but in reality, the basis of their fight was the ability to have their beliefs upheld and respected. They were fighting for their faith.

The actions surrounding this case remind me of the story in John 9. Not focusing on the healing of the man, but the beliefs of all involved. It was believed that only a sinner would perform such an act on the Sabbath. It was believed that the cause of the man's blindness was the result of his parent's sin. At one point, it was believed the man was not born blind. There is an implied belief in security when the man is "abandoned" by his parents and made to stand on his own "belief." They dared not lose their place in the community. Everyone was accustomed to believing what he or she was familiar with. Anything contrary to that, they believed was somehow wrong.

I believe we mean well, in society or medicine, in attempting to preserve life, but the greatest challenge becomes drawing the line between cultural views and spiritual views. The United States government draws many laws on biblical principles, although we may argue about what freedom of religion

---

189 (Lysaught, Kotva Jr and al. 2012), 1129

means. In that same vein, how do we delineate between what is morally ethical and spiritually ethical without imposing on the rights of individuals? There are plenty of cases where spiritual beliefs come in to question. We argue over the right of religious freedom, but in cases like this, how do we not impose on not only the parents' right to believe but their right in how to believe. Some would argue that they should take the baby off the ventilator because that is showing faith. The argument is God does not need a ventilator, and if he is going to revive her, then he would do so without the ventilator. However, what gives us the right to argue this or believe we, as persons, get to determine how and when God will work? If a person believes God can work in various ways, then is it not their right? Is that still not the essence of having faith?

In the end Baby Rena died. Many would argue the family failed, and they were wrong in their beliefs. Others would argue that because healing can come in different ways, Baby Rena was "healed" from her suffering. She no longer has to suffer from her ailments. The parents followed what they believed until the very end of Rena's life. If they had not, what would have been the implications of their ability to heal after her death? While we do not know the answer to this question, the challenge is many do not take this into consideration when considering someone else's decisions in their faith. It is easy to think we have the answers or know better, but the truth is we are often not privy to all the reasons decisions are or must be made. We cannot become so common in our faith or beliefs that we see God moving only linear...one direction.

We cannot tell people how to believe or how God will work in their life. He works in many ways, seen and unseen known and unknown. The key is trusting and having faith that he will do what He says He will do.

Part III

THE LEADERSHIP PERSPECTIVE

The Power of Influence

God will use human relationships to guide us along our journeys and help in spiritual growth.

As a minister, I believe leaders have a powerful influence in the lives of those they are called to lead. Having witnessed and experienced being part of congregations where leaders delivered messages developed more from personal biases, I have witnessed the impact in the lives of their followers. The outcome, for those I have encountered, has resulted in conflicting identity issues. These individuals have struggled with not only identifying what they believed but why they believed. The influences of these leaders impacted their relationship with God and/or how they viewed God.

Leaders have a responsibility to adhere to certain "rules" as they are called by God, representing God's work/will. In return, they should demonstrate certain characteristics realizing how they can influence one's relationship with God. Every aspect of a leader's life influences those around them. This includes accepting responsibility for our actions and motives for their actions. Leaders are expected to lead in honesty and integrity.

The book of kings is full of relevant and practical messages for the newer generations that demonstrate how God uses relationships to guide his people. While much complexity exists among the characters and their stories, there are many lessons to grasp by studying the scriptures. These lessons provide more than the fears of disobedience. They give the reader insight into the God that Elijah identified with. A God that lets his people know they are not forgotten no matter how things may appear.

In Kings, we see the relationship between God and his people as he uses an earthly king to not only lead but provide for the people. God used the prophets to play a significant part in shaping the understanding of God's will for the people as guides in understanding divine perspective. The prophets brought warnings and lessons to the king and the people of the importance of living according to the Deuteronomic code. The key for these kings and people, as it is for us today, is to learn to reign in covenant with God. In turn, we, as godly leaders, take care of God's people.

Let's examine three prophet-king relationships in *Kings*--Nathan-David, unnamed "man of God"-Jeroboam, and Elijah-Ahab--in order to ascertain (a) the circumstances/conflicts drawing them together, (b) how these circumstances/conflicts are resolved (or left unresolved), (c) what the prophetic narrator of *Kings* is saying about God through these stories, and (d) how this Word can be applied to the contemporary Church as it relates to relationships. Closely reviewing these characters, their roles, and relationships, we may identify the power of influence in connecting or leading people to God.

As the relationships of these prophets-kings can be extensive, I will narrow the scope of these relationships. The focus will be on a specific confrontation between each prophet-king.

Nathan-David relationship focuses on II Samuel 12:1-15

1. The unnamed man of God-Jeroboam relationship focuses on I Kings 13:1-10

2. Elijah-Ahab relationship focus on I Kings 21:17-29

Finally, as people encounter numerous influences, I will narrow the scope of application to relationships with church leadership (clergy). Here I will examine the importance of proper influential leadership, how leaders can influence, as well as impacts of negative influences.

Nathan-David: II Samuel 12:1-15 (NRSV)

The conflict:

God sends Nathan to deliver a message to David regarding David's recent accounts/relationship with Bathsheba and Uriah (II Samuel 12:1). The issue Nathan must address is David's sin- Abuse of power leading to acts of adultery and murder. God makes it known he is displeased with David (II Samuel 11:26).

David has taken Bathsheba, the wife of Uriah, and committed adultery. This act alone could suggest an example of a king abusing a subordinate.[190] When Bathsheba becomes pregnant, David devises a plan to cover up his actions. His plan cannot be accomplished alone, and he needs to draw in others to unknowingly participate.

David uses Joab to retrieve Uriah from battle. The king tells Uriah he wants to get updates on the war (II Samuel 11:6-7). David presents the image of a kind, caring, and compassionate king, yet his motifs are contrary to this. His goal is to get Uriah to sleep with his own wife (II Samuel 11:8). This would cover David's active participation in Bathsheba's pregnancy. Unfortunately, for David, Uriah is faithful to his position as a leader. He cares not to indulge in comfort while his men are still in the fields, fighting and living in unfavorable con-

---

190 (Moore 2003), 30

ditions (II Samuel 11:11). The plan derails again, as David portrays the image of a compassionate king inviting Uriah to dine with him. His action again is not compassionate as his goal is to get Uriah drunk enough to sleep with Bathsheba. This fails, too (II Samuel 12-13). In the end, David sets Uriah up to be killed, using Joab (II Samuel 11:14-17). Now, David can take Bathsheba to become his wife and father the child she carries.

God's message, delivered by Nathan, accounts for David's evil actions and the judgment God will deliver. Nathan addresses that the Lord has anointed David as king, given him the house of Israel, and if that were not enough, he (God) would have given David more. There was no excuse to portray such evil and breaking his commandments (II Samuel 12:7-10).

The influence:

Nathan's role cannot be oversimplified. He is to deliver God's message. As we read the passage, it is clear God sent Nathan to David (II Samuel 12:1). As the rest of the events unfold, we witness Nathan's delivery. He first tells David a story, a parable that portrays the events and behavior of a powerful man taking advantage of another. Enraged by the events and the character's actions, David sees fit a rightful judgment. Then, the hammer drops as Nathan identifies David as the character in the story. He is the one who abused power.

We are not privy to the exact directions God provided to Nathan to deliver the message. We can witness the impact of the delivery. We witness how Nathan was able to get David to understand God's message and take responsibility for his actions. We witnessed Nathan's role in getting David to go before or turn to God (II Samuel 12:13) then move out of the way.

As a messenger, commissioned by God, Nathan is provided authority to deliver the word. If it is his choice to deliver it, beginning with a story to get David to identify his sin, he does not actually manipulate David. His actions and behavior are contrary to those portrayed by the king. Nathan has demonstrated the power of influence while remaining within his limitations.

THE LEADERSHIP PERSPECTIVE

The unnamed man of God, from Judah-Jeroboam: I Kings 13:1-10

The conflict:

Jeroboam has sinned and led the people to sin as well. He formalized a personal cult out of his own heart, redefining his kingdom with his own rules. All actions are contrary to the directions given and promises made between him and YHWH. YHWH promises that Jeroboam will be king over Israel, providing he keeps YHWH's statutes and commandments (I Kings 11:35-38).

Jeroboam focused on his personal desires, devises a means to safeguard his promised kingdom. He erects gold calves for Israel to worship. He reinstitutes illegitimate high places,[191] rather than lead the people to worship in YHWH's commissioned temple in Jerusalem. Jeroboam also builds an altar where he would offer sacrifices, which is beyond the scope of his authority as a king.

Message:

The man of God comes to deliver the Lord's message, not directly to Jeroboam but on the altar. From a literary perspective, the altar embodies Jeroboam's, disobedient heart.[192] Jeroboam responds to the man of God and attempts to have him apprehended (I Kings 13:4). Jeroboam loses not only his outstretched hand but also his precious altar, now torn down with the ashes of sacrifices spilled.[193] Concerned for himself, the king attempts to regain what was and will be lost as he asks the prophet to seek the Lord for him. To Jeroboam, the

---

191 (Chung 2010), 28
192 (Wray Beal 2014), 192
193 (Wray Beal 2014), 192

restoral of his hand would symbolize a return of power as well.[194] His hand is restored, yet not his kingdom, like Jeroboam's heart, remained unchanged and committed only to his personal desires.

Influence:

The man of God came to proclaim against the altar, the word of the Lord (I Kings 13:2). Though attacked by Jeroboam, the prophet did not address the message to Jeroboam, as this was not his commission. During the conflict, we witness the prophet act within the confines of his authority and instructions. Jeroboam attempts to sway the prophet to dine with him, which is symbolic of an honor bestowed upon kings, priests, and prophets.[195] The prophet refuses. Unlike Jeroboam, the man of God does not desire to be exalted rather desires to follow the instructions given by God.

Elijah-Ahab: I Kings 21:17-29

The conflict:

God commissions Elijah to address Ahab's sin, "selling himself into evil"[196] (I Kings 21:25). Ahab has committed murder to take the inheritance (land) of Naboth, for his personal gain: a vegetable garden. Furthermore, following his wife, Jezebel, Ahab has allowed Jezebel to conduct such matters disguised under religious authority.

Initially, he attempts to buy Naboth's land. Refusing to sell, Ahab sulks. His wife takes matters into her own hands to obtain the land. Using a trial under the false pretense of YHWH's laws and statues, she has Naboth stoned for false

---

194 (Wray Beal 2014), 192
195 (Wray Beal 2014), 191
196 (Moore 2003), 39

charges. Naboth is accused of cursing God and the king (I Kings 21:8-13). After his death, Jezebel tells Ahab to take Naboth's land as he is now dead. (I Kings 21:15-16).

Like David, Ahab's sin is an abuse of royal power.[197] He, too, is more concerned with his desires rather than anyone else. The difference is Ahab does not initiate the actions of David, yet he does not question the motives or actions of his wife. He is only happy to get what he desired. Beal points out that motifs shape this chapter.[198]

Elijah is sent to deliver the Lord's message to Ahab as he sits in Naboth's garden. Elijah delivers the message, confronting what Ahab has taken against covenant provisions.[199] Ahab turned land meant for one thing (inheritance) and diminished it into something less valued (a garden).[200] The king has allowed influential power to draw others into an evil plan, using the law as the foundation of the charade. The result of his actions and influence caused Israel to sin, just as he has sinned.

In each scenario, we see the role the prophets portrayed to influence each king. Primarily they confront the actions of these kings though the methods were different. We witnessed the actions of each king. As each king falls away from acting as representatives of YHWH, he sends the prophet with a message. The messages address the sins of each king but also within each method, the king is allowed an opportunity to (1) acknowledge their sins, (2) seek the Lord, and (3) repent or change their heart. Just as important, YHWH points out

---

197 (Wray Beal 2014), 272
198 (Wray Beal 2014), 272
199 (Wray Beal 2014), 273
200 (Wray Beal 2014), 274

not only the individual sin but the impact of their actions on others.

Today, as leaders, we can see God's messages to the kings as messages to still abide by. In the stories, we see the relationships of - God: messenger: recipient portrayed as God: Prophet: King.

Today the parallel relationships are- Bible (God's Word): Clergy: Congregation. Leaders are instrumental in leading people to God or shaping their image/relationship with God. Our actions and messages we deliver have a profound impact on those we are speaking to. Our actions in delivering messages should follow the characteristics of the prophets.

"A careful study of these men is sure to influence us to model our lives by their standards, developing a sterner conception of moral behavior, and show the importance of Godly conduct."[201] As leaders demonstrating godly standards we can help others lead a stronger healthier relationship with God. Based on the prophets' messages to the kings, it appears this is God's expectation of his entrusted leaders.

Encountering The Word

It is important to read the words of the Bible and hear the voice of God.[202] We are to think with the scriptures not about them, therefore, keeping the integrity of the author's message. Just as the prophets were the interpreters, leaders of today are as well. We see each prophet demonstrate the importance of holding God's Word in high regard. As God speaks to leaders, today, through the Bible, we are to do the same. "To see the word of scripture and sacrament as an icon is to

---

201 (Yates 1942), 1
202 (Green 2007), 41

believe that God is present in an incarnational way; coming at us in the manner of Jesus."[203] We are to see God's words coming to us in God's loving promises and actions demonstrated in Israel, embodied in Jesus, and passed down to the church.[204]

Delivering Messages

As each prophet delivered the messages to the kings, they demonstrated the opposite behavior of the king. They exemplified what each king should have done. The same should be demonstrated when delivering messages today. It is important for clergy to demonstrate the ability to read Bible stories from the perspective of the author rather than applying them to themselves. In return, we influence laity demonstrating the importance to learn basic principles to contextual interpretation of scripture.[205] The results should be people experiencing the truth that changes their lives from the inside out.[206]

Misusing the Word

Feeding desires such as maintaining relevancy, power, and control can cause a leader to self-destruct when faced with uncontrolled values, needs, and pressures.[207] It is possible that some leaders teach the word for personal gain rather than to heal and to set free. As David Johnson identifies reasons for misusing the word, I have identified how it relates to the characteristics and actions of each discussed king. He states that misusing the word is used to drive others for a variety of reasons such as, to keep others from holding them

---

203 (Bolsinger 2004), 125
204 (Bolsinger 2004), 125
205 (Powell 2007), 92
206 (Johnson and Vonderen 1991), 152
207 (Heifetz and Linsky 2002), 152

accountable (Jeroboam), to protect their image (David), to uphold doctrine they have based a whole ministry upon (Ahab-Jezebel), to keep funds coming in (Jeroboam, Ahab), to build religious kingdoms in order to bolder their own spiritual self-esteem (Jeroboam).

The impact is abusive systems like the abuse frowned upon by God as witnessed in the prophets' messages. Such abusive systems employ unhealthy relationship skills "for God" rather than taking the "painful course of receiving help to change them."[208]

Living by Example

"Christian faith is about relationship and not just a laundry list of things to do."[209] Every aspect of a leader's life influences those around them. This includes accepting responsibility for our actions. In each of the prophet's message, they showed the kings the role they played in the lives of others. In David's interaction with Uriah, he demonstrated qualities of compassion to his subordinate. His actions portrayed and what he attempted to accomplish were hypocritical of each other. The same applied to Jeroboam as he tells the people they no longer must travel the distance to Jerusalem to worship. Instead, he created high places for them to worship. Both kings had ulterior motives for their actions. Leaders are expected to lead in honesty and integrity.

Jesus often criticized how deep-seated hypocrisy produces spiritual barricades.[210] Research, from the Barna Group, has

---

208 (Johnson and Vonderen 1991), 196

209 (Kinnaman, You Lost Me: Why Young Christians Are Leaving The Church...And Rethinking Faith 2011), 164

210 (Kinnaman, You Lost Me: Why Young Christians Are Leaving The Church...And Rethinking Faith 2011), 43

shown that hypocrisy has been partly responsible for separating the younger generation from the purposes of God in their lives.[211] If we are to lead people to better relationships with God, we must demonstrate those behaviors that guide those relationships. Every aspect of our lives shows others what God is like."[212]

"Churches are shaped by habits, which are shaped over decades and centuries by the interaction of reflection and action. Our individual habits and biases are shaped by the habits of the group, whether the group is our church or some other identifiable social influence."

As leaders, we have a great deal of influence in the lives of those we lead. How we deliver the word, verbally and through our actions affect the relationships our followers develop with God. The image we portray in our actions and our engagement with God's Word influences the image followers develop about God. It is vital that we understand the power of our influences. We have examples of the kings to demonstrate the effectiveness of influence and how not to abuse them. We are also provided with examples from the prophets on how to properly utilize our influence. In examining the prophet-king relationships, we can learn how to properly use our influences as well as what God expects from us as leaders and why.

---

[211] (Kinnaman, You Lost Me: Why Young Christians Are Leaving The Church...And Rethinking Faith 2011), 44
[212] (Kinnaman and Lyons, Unchristian: What A New Generation Really Thinks About Christianity 2007), 36

The Honor Code

The key to the future is understanding God's ongoing commitment to His people, in spite of any and everything. He will do whatever it takes to remind of us this commitment, which speaks to His Love and our worth and purpose. The circumstances and conflicts surrounding the rise of Abimelech compared to Gideon is an example of the great lengths God will take to remind us of the historical covenant and promise to us all, to have a live fulfilled with Him.

In Judges 9: 1-2, Abimelech, in comparison makes a similar decision as his father in Judges 6:25 to separate himself from his father. The axis point that separates Yahweh's Champion from the people's king, seems to be the motive behind the decision that drives the division. For Gideon, he is commissioned by the Lord to take part in the plan of delivering God's people (Judges 6:14). Abimelech's motives are far contrary, as he works to essentially strengthen the power of idolatry in the region that will put God's people in captivity. As we examine the crossroads for both Abimelech and Gideon, we would see a parallel in the decision by the people of Israel to follow God. Furthermore, the characters twined together provide insight into the narrator's inclusion of this story as a reminder of the historical events surrounding the exodus, which are vital to the relationship between Yahweh and his people.

As we further examine the text, I will argue that this word speaks to the contemporary church today regarding our decisions and interactions with Christ. I will argue that much like the covenant people of yesterday, part of the family today, God will still show an ongoing commitment to his people despite everything so that they can have a future with him. This is also impacted by God's chosen leaders' commitment to follow and effectively lead people in the way of Christ.

I. Judges 9:15-19 - Question of Alignments

There are significant agreements that are challenged in this text: the Abimelech-Shechemites Alliance with undertones of Gideon's message for the people to have only God as ruler (Judges 8:23), and the structural narrative that plays to the events in Joshua 24:1, calling attention to Israel affirming their covenant to Yahweh.

A. Issue of Kingship

"15 And the bramble said to the trees, 'If in good faith you are anointing me king over you, then come and take refuge in my shade; but if not, let fire come out of the bramble and devour the cedars of Lebanon.' 16 "Now therefore, if you acted in good faith and honor when you made Abimelech king, and if you have dealt well with Jerubbaal and his house, and have done to him as his actions deserved" (Judges 9:15-16).

The circumstances surrounding the agreement between Abimelech and the Shechemites are challenged, but research implies them to be disloyal to the past actions of both Yahweh and Gideon and thereby show the future intent of Abimelech's rule.

Judges did not receive an inherited seat or position of authority solely through an agreement of the people. Rather they often received their authority, as a leader when the spirit of the Lord descended upon them.[213] After that, knowing Yahweh was with them, they would move forward with a sense of power and urgency and the people would follow.

Abimelech's rise to power in the most nontraditional way affirms by definition his appointment. He is neither a judge nor deliverer; he is a king selected by the people (Judges 9:3). He is not commissioned by Yahweh neither directly nor through the means of one of Yahweh's messengers. He is the first reign in succession of his father although his actions show he has no intentions to honor any legacy of his father. His election is contrary to the agreement or mandate called by Gideon to allow no one in his lineage to rule over the people, but only Yahweh to rule is dishonored (Judges 8:23).

B. Forged Alliance

"17. for my father fought for you, and risked his life, and rescued you from the hand of Midian; 18. but you have risen up against my father's house this day, and have killed his sons, seventy men on one stone, and have made Abimelech, the son of his slave woman, king over the lords of Shechem, because he is your kinsman—" (Judges 9:17-18)

Jotham's accusations speak to his father's, Gideon, heroic acts on behalf of the people of Shechem to deliver them from Midian (Judges 9:17). With the implicit acts committed against his family, killing his brothers "seventy-men-on-one-stone," Jotham's brother (Judges 9:18), Abimelech, has made a conscious decision to turn against his father's family for the favoritism and alliance of his mother's, (the concubine's people) (Judges 9:1-2) to make him their king (Judges 9:6).

---

213 Richard Alter, *Ancient Israel: The Former Prophets* (New York: W.W. Norton & Company, 2013), 106

Abimelech's claim to fame is validated by the lords of Shechem (Judges 9:3; 9:6) thanks to his manipulating actions to assume power. Roger Ryan, in his *Judges* commentary, would argue that Abimelech's actions characterize him as an impatient king in waiting.[214] This claim makes sense when supported by Gale Yee's social scientific criticism perspective, in *Judges &Method: New Approaches in Biblical Studies*. She implies that Abimelech's actions suggest he is acting with power, but without legitimate authority, for he is disloyal to the ancient Israelite societal norms of patrilineal kinship.[215]

C. False Power

"They gave him seventy pieces of silver out of the temple of Baal-berith with which Abimelech hired worthless and reckless fellows, who followed him. ⁵ He went to his father's house at Ophrah, and killed his brothers the sons of Jerubbaal, seventy men, on one stone; but Jotham, the youngest son of Jerubbaal, survived, for he hid himself. ⁶ Then all the lords of Shechem and all Beth-millo came together, and they went and made Abimelech king, by the oak of the pillar at Shechem." (Judges 9:4-7)

Historically the narrator recorded a Judge's commission through a sequence of actions which are not followed in the narrative of Abimelech. As Yahweh's unwritten commissioning rules implied by previous patterns are absent in Abimelech's appointment, this would imply a blatant intent of disloyalty and future plans of dishonorable covenant.

---

214 Roger Ryan, *Judges* (Sheffield: Sheffield Phoenix Press, 2007), 68

215 Gale Yee, *Judges & Methods: New Approaches in Biblical Studies* (Minneapolis: Fortress Press, 2007), 58

Yahweh is the overseer or God of the covenants for the commission of Judges, and Abimelech's commission is sanctioned by Baal-Berith, a Shechemite deity, confirming its illegality. When we compare the preset before the rise to power of Abimelech and Gideon, there is no divine interaction (directly or implied) on behalf of Yahweh. Rather the Shechemite lords pay Abimelech from the treasure of Baal-berith. Theodore Lewis' research notes this Canaanite deity as, the "god of the covenant" or divine witness/guardian of the treaty.[216] The role, in such a situation, is to witness the agreement between human parties, which, is contrary to covenants made between Yahweh and the human. Perhaps, the foundation of this treaty made solely between humans and not with humans and Yahweh speaks to a greater issue. Lewis would contend this patron deity only witnessed oaths, implying it gave no authority compared to the authority received in a Judges' commission by Yahweh. With his stance, I would further conclude Abimelech's authority was not given but taken.

II. The Final Covenant Reminder

"Then all the lords of Shechem and all Beth-Millo came together, and they went and made Abimelech king, by the oak of the pillar at Shechem. When it was told to Jotham, he went and stood on the top of Mount Gerizim, and cried aloud and said to them, "Listen to me, you lords of Shechem, so that God may listen to you" (Judges 9:6-7).

Yee implies that as we study narrative criticism elements such as the setting the narrator emphasis, this helps to provide thematic unity and coherence to the conventions of an-

---

[216] Theodore Lewis, "The Identity and Function of El/Baal Berith," Journal of Biblical Literature, 1996, 416

cient Hebrew narrative.[217] The Judge's narrator is specific in offering detailed location in this story which supports the idea that these are vital to a deeper understanding or connection with, perhaps, the characters historical context.

Jotham's cry is atop of Mount Gerizim (Judges 9:7) would imply his forthcoming speech would be more than a connection of understanding the parable but pointing to the connection of the location with the people below him and perhaps, Yahweh above him. With the circumstances and conflicts surrounding Abimelech's rise to power and the loyalty towards Gideon at the foundation of this appeal, I contend that the location adds the tension of who or what god will govern the people.

The location of the new king has been dedicated to Yahweh since the established covenant between Abram and Yahweh, though the narrator's detailed accounts surround Abimelech's new appointment and ties to the location would tend to argue his blatant disregard for the historical covenant which impacts the future of the people. When "Abram passed through the land to the place at Shechem, to the oak of Moreh. At that time the Canaanites were in the land. Then the Lord appeared to Abram, and said, "To your offspring I will give this land." So he built there an altar to the Lord, who had appeared to him" (Genesis 12:6-7). The same location continues to be prominent in Israel's patriarchal history, that scholars noted it is the "capital of political and religious prominence."[218] This same location is where Jacob purchased land from the "the sons of Hamor" again, built an altar to Yahweh (Genesis 35:1-4) and his clan "engaged in ritual acts (purifi-

---

217 Yee, Judges & Methods, 29
218 Bernhard W. Anderson, "The Place of Shechem in the Bible," The American Schools of Oriental Research, 1957, 10

cation, change of garments, burial of idols and ear-rings beneath the Oak of Moreh."[219] Furthermore, in Joshua 24, after the initial (promised) success in Canaan, Joshua "assembled the Hebrew tribes at Shechem 'before God', near the Oak of Moreh."[220] He recited the story of Yahweh's mighty acts made known especially in the Exodus and the victories against the Amorites. He summoned the people to put away their foreign gods. The people affirmed their covenant to Yahweh by responding, "Far be it from us that we should forsake the LORD to serve other gods; for it is the LORD our God who brought us and our ancestors up from the land of Egypt, out of the house of slavery, and who did those great signs in our sight. He protected us along all the way that we went, and among all the peoples through whom we passed; ¹⁸and the LORD drove out before us all the peoples, the Amorites who lived in the land. Therefore, we also will serve the LORD, for he is our God" (Joshua 24:16-18).

They erected a stone beneath the Oak of Moreh as "Joshua said to all the people, 'See, this stone shall be a witness against us; for it has heard all the words of the LORD that he spoke to us; therefore, it shall be a witness against you, if you deal falsely with your God'" (Joshua 24:27).

Their previous commitment has sealed their future relationship and fate with Yahweh. No matter what occurs they will continue to be his people and He will continue to be their God. Therefore, as Mount Gerizim is significant to Jotham's patriarchal history his speech here, speaks to Jotham's honorable ties not just to his father, but he remembers the covenant they made between his father's people and Yahweh. Unlike his brother, Abimelech, whose loyalty is in question,

---

219 Anderson, "The Place of Shechem in the Bible," 11
220 Anderson, "The Place of Shechem in the Bible," 14

he climbs Mount Gerizim, known as a place of blessings and curses, to seek justice in the form of a blessing or a curse on the disloyal parties. I would further argue that Jotham may perhaps be taking a parallel stance, a Joshua-like character as well, as his words will ultimately affect not only the Shechemites and Abimelech, but also all of Israel.

Judges 9:22-23 Judgement

Ryan suggests a pattern Yahweh uses to sell the people of Israel into the hands of unruly kings to discipline them for their disobedience.[221] This would seem to support the allowance for Abimelech to "rule over Israel for three years" before Yahweh intervenes despite Jotham's cry for justice. It seems justice was brought to all of Israel, not just Abimelech and the lords of Shechem, but leaves the question of why. After all, if Jotham has cried out for the honor of his father and his brother, why would Yahweh not just bring immediate retribution?

Ryan argues that Abimelech, the "opportunist"[222] leader, has exploited the kinship of his (mother and) father strictly as a power move. I would argue that the opportunity must be present for one to exploit it therefore, it would seem to imply Israel's fallen state prior to Abimelech's rise to power. Preceding Abimelech's powerplay, the Judge's narrator points out a period of apostasy during Gideon's period as Judge. Ryan implies that Gideon's retirement came before he died, due to his involvement in Israel's backslidden state of idolatry [223] (Judges 8:28-29), though initially struggling with this implication, I would agree with the argument. Gideon's in-

---

221 Ryan, *Judges,* 17
222 Ryan, *Judges,*67
223 Ryan, *Judges,* 63

volvement in constructing the ephod which "all of Israel prostituted themselves to" (Judges 8:27), was parallel to Aaron constructing the golden calf for Israel (Exodus 32). This action angered God (Deuteronomy 9), but the actions are mitigated thanks to Moses' mediation on Aaron's behalf. [224] This could suggest Jotham's position and speech could also act as mediation for his father's actions and perhaps invoking the missing Israel cry that normally precedes the rise of a Judge.

The allowed time Israel is under the earthly king's, Abimelech, rule rather than Yahweh, would seem to correlate with Ryan's "selling" argument and the Joshua 24 covenant renewal ritual. Part of the agreement, in Joshua 24 was the Hebrew people's understanding that they could not serve other gods for the Lord was a holy and jealous God and would not forgive their transgressions or sins (Joshua 24:19); "If you forsake the LORD and serve foreign gods, then he will turn and do you harm, and consume you, after having done you good" (Joshua 24:20). Therefore, the people are reminded of their transgressions by Yahweh invoking justice in the very place the covenant was invoked and the people made their commitment to him. The stronger statement would imply he has kept his part of the past covenant, and even their captivity would in fact be his continued commitment to it and them, despite the people's continued transgressions.

Their past is being reconciled with their present which will impact their future, as Shechem will also become the place in Israel's future monarch history. Shechem becomes the point where the people once made a dedication to serving only God, but later would continue to be where the (ill-famed) northern monarchies would rule, which kings were appointed by pop-

---

224 James W. Watts, "Aaron and the Golden Calf in the Rhetoric of the Pentateuch," The Society of Biblical Literature, 2011,42

ulace or popularity[225] similar to Abimelech rather through a commitment with Yahweh, where rules are set in place to govern appointments. The future appointments by popular acclaim rather than those who are committed to the laws of Yahweh, would continue to have destructive consequences for Israel, just as Moses warned in Deuteronomy 17:14-20.

III. Contemporary Application

Abimelech's story, while set in the Old Testament speaks a relevant message to today's society and the contemporary church. The story speaks to how some of the challenges we face in our everyday life and how we decide to respond, impact how we see and feel about God.

When faced with challenges of life, we, like Gideon, at the crossroad of his commission may wonder, where is God? How or why has he abandoned you in a time of dire need? If he is such a faithful God, then how has he forgotten about you? As we reflect upon the circumstances surrounding the rise of both Abimelech and Gideon, as well as the experiences of Yahweh's chosen people, I would contend that God has never forgotten about any of his people. Perhaps, as we have focused so much on what God has not done, which may skew how we see him, we may be inclined to refocus on what we can do in support of our situations.

Israel's history reminds us of Yahweh's established covenant with Abram in Genesis 17. While God made promises to Abram, God makes known what he expects from Abram as part of the covenant terms. As the covenant affects Abram's present and future, Yahweh includes the future generations

---

225 Brian P. Irwin, "Not Just Any King: Abimelech, the Northern Monarchy, and the Final Form of Judges," Journal of Biblical Literature, 2012, 450

in the terms of the covenant contract. "God said to Abraham, 'As for you, you shall keep my covenant, you and your offspring after you throughout their generations" (Genesis 17:9). This would imply why each patriarch leader passed down the people's history, as a continued reminder that while God would always be there God, they also had a responsibility to live with him or keep their end of the agreement.

Later, after the Exodus Moses would pass down the laws, ordinances, and statues given by God for the people so they "may know that I am Lord your God" (Deuteronomy 29:5). This would give further detailed accounts on how to "succeed in everything that you do", in the future (Deuteronomy 29:9) if they were diligent in their observance. Several times again, including Joshua's assembly in Joshua 24, the people are reminded to put nothing between them and the Lord their God. They are encouraged to commit to following Yahweh and reminded of all He has done for them since the beginning of their history. At that moment, a conscious decision was made as the people put away their idols and committed to serving only Yahweh. It is believed, due to their continued idolatrous backslidings they did not fully understand the meaning behind their commitment [226] as the words rolled easily off their tongues. Nonetheless, the deal is sealed as Joshua reaffirms before the Lord what they commit and how the Lord will respond to their transgressions.

What we have learned is the guilty party in the continuous breaking of the covenant are the people, not God. They have continuously fashioned anything and everything between themselves and Yahweh despite his continued commitment to provide and rescue them. Yet, the only one everyone blames is God, there is no self-accountability for their actions

---

226 Alter, *Ancient Israel*, 10

or lack thereof as implied by Yahweh's response to Israel's cry in Judges 6:7-9. The Lord's prophet reminds the people all the Lord has done to provide and rescue them since their enslavement in Egypt, yet the people have paid reverence to the gods of the Amorites and not heeded the Lord's voice.

Turning back to today's church and the secular society, I would say this is the same problem. While we cannot ignore the trouble, we see daily, I would argue there seems to be a shortfall in the area of self-accountability for it, instead, the overall church and God seems to be the blame. No contention is made regarding what "I can change."

In Genesis 17:1, the Lord tells Abram to be blameless (or innocent of wrongdoing) when he establishes his covenant with him. Eventually we learn that throughout Israelite history, no one is completely innocent of wrongdoing, but we do see where God mitigates or forgives when there is mediation (and/or repentance). Moses mediated on behalf of Aaron (Deuteronomy 9), perhaps Jotham on behalf of Gideon Judges 9), and today we have Christ who mediates on our behalf. Yet, that does not absolve us of responsibilities in serving and following the ways of Christ. As Peter instructs the exiles of the Dispersion in Pontus, Galatia, Cappadocia, Asia and Bithynia who have been chosen by God, to live as servants of God by following the example Christ led (I Peter 1-2), I would contend we too, should be making the sacrifices to walk in his footsteps.

We cannot expect much while giving little or nothing then expect to partake in the promises of Christ for our future. Through Christ, we are given a life of hope birthed through his resurrection, and heirs of "an inheritance that is imperishable, undefiled and unfading, kept in heaven for you, who are being protected by the power of God through faith for a salvation ready in the last time" (I Peter 4-5). Yet, this precludes there is the responsibility on the part of the individuals attempting to covet a relationship with him.

As we are called by God to join him in the committed mission of providing and protecting his people, it is important to understand that just as we witnessed the axis point in which Abimelech and Gideon made decisions on how to lead, we too are held accountable for our actions. The implication of the commission as his people, especially leaders, is the same as past Judges, in that we must not compromise the integral authority by which we are given. By placing anything between what we are called to do and God, we take the risk of becoming the institutions that fail to provide stability and instead become ineffective and harmful because of moral bankruptcy. We become part of the hindrance, which causes the people to see God and live with God ineffectively.

How Are You Leading?

Henri Nouwen's, In the Name of Jesus, explores Christian Leadership as he tells of his personal growth during his move from Harvard to L'Arche. The author transparently tells of preconceived ideas of ministerial leadership and how this was changed during his time spent living among the mentally handicapped. Nouwen discussed these lessons as he breaks down each preconceived idea that not only plagued him but many other leaders. These areas are divided into discussions of the problematic areas of relevancy, popularity, and leading, directing the reader to understand the more important factors of prayer, ministry, and being led.

In the Name of Jesus, was an interesting read. One that would make sense to share with anyone entering early in ministry and any other role of leadership. The further I continued to read, however, I kept wondering about the examples he had to emulate as lessons learned appeared rather basic, to me.

Nouwen points to the importance of a leader dealing with aspirations of his own ministry. As he describes one major issue or suffering in ministry: low self-esteem,[227] I somewhat wondered if relevancy and low self-esteem coincided. It makes sense as he explains the dilemma of not feeling one is making an impact or perhaps the impact, they believed they

---

227 (Nowen 1989), 31

should be making. I agree with his thought that, "the Christian Leader is called to be irrelevant offering his vulnerable self. [228] I see the issue as having a false idea of what impact one is supposed to make. Perhaps my disadvantage, in reading this material, is that I have spent over two decades leading people after continued leadership training, mentoring, failures, learning from past mistakes, and teaching/grooming other leaders. This does not make me an expert nor one who proclaims to not make continued mistakes. I do wonder how after 25 years the issue of relevancy appears with him in this manner. After 25 years, the lesson of realizing the importance of prayer and having a deep personal (intimate) relationship with God is now a "revelation?" I was struck a little by this.

Similar thoughts and questions struck me moving forward in the lesson of "From Popularity to Ministry," dealing with individualism. I spent years attempting to deny or run from the call to ministry mostly due to witnessing the challenges and sacrifices of others, over the years. I struggle with understanding ideas for desires of ministry popularity. Nouwen mentions that many "feel like failed tightrope walkers who discovered that we did not have the power to draw thousands of people…"[229] How or why the great "self" expectation in the first place? This is not looking pessimistically but even with a desire to do great things, the way we accomplish or measure great is often times skewed. The smallest victories are many times the greatest feat. We have to see the beauty in that.

When I think of Jesus on the cross with so many standing before Him witnessing and all those who left Him or chanted for His persecution, I look at the two criminals on either side

---

228 (Nowen 1989), 30
229 (Nowen 1989), 25

of Him. One scoffed like the others watching, even as he was dying but the other defended Jesus saying he has done nothing wrong and asked that Jesus would remember him (Luke 23:39-43). See, this is the ONE we should see. This is a victory, not the crowds. There can be greater impact in the one we reach than the thousands who come merely to spectate in a room. We see numbers but that does not equate to impact and victory. Furthermore, identifying ministry as a form of individualistic heroism is far from anything we learn from Jesus as He taught the disciples.

Nouwen shares his experience of boarding in this community, realizing the importance of communal and mutual ministry experience and dispels the idea that "good leadership require a safe distance from those we are called to lead."[230] He stresses the important of relationships. This is similar to leadership lessons in the military. There you understand that without trust and communication you cannot begin to expect one to follow as they do not know their leader. The top down approach rather than a sometimes-lateral leadership method is not conducive to all situations. Part of understanding leadership is knowing that it is not about power and control.

Sometimes you can spend a countless hours with a person praying with them, for them, mentoring them, pouring into them, taking "hits" for and from them, etc. and while they will never publicly share this with others, yet send accolades, shout outs, happy birthday messages, public support for various things they are never ashamed to stand behind in the public eye, we must stay loyal and faithful to what God has placed us in their life to do, no matter the cost.

---

230 (Nowen 1989), 61

We must hold our position God places us in, even when "shots are fired," when they manifest and fight back in rebellion and retaliation because this fight is for their purpose and their destiny. We must remember we are standing, holding firm for what God has shown us is ahead for them...what the adversary does not want them to reach. The battle, this fight is not about us. We must not take anything personally. Instead we must discern the spirit that is at work trying to hold them locked down in a place where they do not belong. We must recognize the spirit that is attempting to keep them in bondage, enslaved and trapped. When we keep our eyes on The Lord and follow the guidance of the Holy Spirit, we can discern accurately, thus provide direction, love, grace, and mercy allowing them to still see HOPE. For, if we take our eyes off of the Lord, we lose the inability to see who they are as The Father sees them. Therefore, we lose the inability to see HOPE for their future and become advocates in their bondage, enslavement, and death of their soul. So, as we are called to lead, we must also remember that we are called to lead in LOVE. That means that love is unconditional, and we stand...stand strong, fighting for the present and future we are entrusted with no matter the cost. We must be willing to put it all on the line for the lives we are assigned.

You think the life of Christ was just an example for all Christians to follow just in generality? Take a closer look and see another perspective. The perspective of a leader. The leader who showed us how to teach, love, mentor, guide, and raise disciples while giving all of himself yet wanting nothing for himself. He gave up EVERYTHING for EVERYONE, even those who did not believe in Him, but He believed in them. As He hung high on the cross, which stood high on Golgotha where he could see all of those below, not just through his vision, but through the eyes of the Father, He saw a void that needed filling. He sought mercy for all who stood before Him. He did not look simply on the outside, but rather who they were and what was going on inside and what was keeping them from moving forward.

The challenge we have with moving forward is what our minds comprehend and what our eyes see. What Christ would show us is that as we are drawn close...closer to The Father, giving up ourselves, willing to sacrifice everything, coming out of our natural minds and our natural vision, taking the mind and vision of The Father, we gain a greater perspective. So, here He is, on the cross which is on Golgotha, "the place of the skull." Keep in mind two major functions of the skull is to protect the brain and the eyes. These two organs we use to literally see the world around us, as we make judgment calls on what to do, when, and how to do it. As we walk through life leaning on our understanding, where does this lead us?

Many times, we are walking around troubled, confused, worried about how things will work. We have highs and lows because one-day things work and the next day, we are unsure if it will, again. Our moods are inconsistent because they are based on situations and circumstances, what we can see and what we cannot. When we operate this way, we wonder why we have difficulty leading and teaching those we come in contact with. We wonder why we have difficulty or inconsistency leading those who are sent to us. It is because we are trusting in what we see and what we understand. We are trusting in what seems to be "normal." We forget the demonstrative leadership example Christ gave us in His ultimate sacrifice.

We simplify His sacrifice to the "Easter" type messages we give to the general congregations about how Christ died so we all could live and have everlasting life. Yet, we forget that whenever we are given a message, it is first meant for us. We forget that as we study intensely, we gain the greater message that speaks to us to build us and push us forward. This must happen before we give the shorter and more focused version to the general public or congregation. I fail to understand how leaders walk into a space believing the same message for the sheep was also for the Shepherd. As one who is leading should your message be of greater substance to help nurture you where you are and not drinking the exact same formula as the rest of the sheep? Honestly, even the sheep do not eat the exact same meal as a lamb. Babies are unable to digest what adult eats. So why, as a leader, are we watering down the Word for our consumption? How is that helping us grow? How is that helping those we are entrusted to serve, grow?

We want to grow; we must be willing to give something up. We must be willing to follow Christ. Really follow Christ. We must be willing to do whatever it takes, no matter the cost. When Jesus prayed on the Mount of Olives, before he was arrested, he asked, " Father if you are willing remove this cup from me; yet not my will but yours be done" (Luke 32:42). While He understood what was coming was not something we would have "selfishly" volunteered for, would cost Him a great deal, and would rather this not be the case, he says yet not my will but yours be done. Meaning, this is not about me, not about my personal wants, needs or desires, but about my Father's will and I will surrender everything for that. And so He did. When He committed, help was sent to provide Him the strength He needed for what was immediately coming. Help was provided along the way, when He became weak, beaten and tormented by chastisers, accusers, naysayers, and tormentors. He was able to withstand the harshest treatment that we all cringe and cry when reading about or seeing portrayed in dramatized events. Even through it all, when on that cross, beaten, bruised, whipped, nailed, He hung at a high point, over the people. Not in a place of honor but in a place of humility and high above the place of the skull, closer to the Father where vision is not obscured. He SEES.

He SEES who is really broken. He SEES who is really hurt. He SEES who really needs help and it is not Him. It is those below. Those who in their audible, previously cried crucify him. Those who in their audible mocked and were scornful but the soul cried out pain and suffering from being trapped in their own understanding. The suffering of being stuck in a place with obscured vision. Stuck in a place where hope was not visualized. Stuck in a place where greater was unimaginable. Stuck in a state of unbelief. Stuck in a state…Just stuck…

So, understanding what Mercy is, He says, "Father forgive them for they do not know what they are doing" (Luke 23:34).

Mercy is a gift. A precious gift. One that was given to us all, and thus we must continue to give what has been given to us. It comes at a cost. It takes a sacrifice and that sacrifice, first is giving up self, your ways, your will, your understanding, and your vision and taking on that which belongs to The Father. As we allow ourselves to become stripped of everything, so we can be raised up and drawn closer to The Father…allowing Him to bring us outside the ways of what our natural mind and eyes would normally comprehend, then we can begin to see the world, His creation and created beings through His eyes. We begin to see them for who He created them to be, therefore begin to gain greater insight to lead them down the path He designed for them. When they begin to rebel or retaliate, we won't take it personal. When they fail to cooperate, become difficult, or never acknowledge whatever work you have done or continue to do for them, you will not become unraveled. Instead, you will remain calm and know that because of these actions, you must be on the right back and they are getting closer to another stage in their victorious journey. Celebrate the challenges as that means progress is taking place and you have been following God, therefore hell is not happy. Do not leave your post, for this is not the time to give up. Instead...PRAISE.

Give God all the PRAISE, in JESUS name. This is where you have no MERCY and take no prisoners...In YOUR PRAISE. The Power of your Praise will give you strength to pull through the next phase as you help lead others to live life in Purpose and on Purpose

Welcome to the MERCY Seat!

As leaders, especially in ministry, we often teach how important it is to love those we are called to lead, but we miss how critical the gift of Mercy is to life and future of those we are called to. As believers, we look at who we consider "others," misjudging because of what we believe. The truth is we have failed to see them the way we needed to. We leaned our understanding and our vision, rather than surrendering our everything to take on the mind, heart, and vision of The Father so that we may SEE His created beings as he made them.

Even as Christ had been beaten, tormented, and crucified, He hung there high over the people in humility and in a place where He could see from His Father's perspective those who were in a greater need than He. Then He hung there, in His "brokenness" between The Father and those below seeking MERCY on behalf of the truly broken and hurting.

He is not focused on himself, what has happened to Him, and the people below most who are the reason He is there suffering. Instead, He focuses on what is really going on. They are in a place of suffering well beyond any pain that He is experiencing. Why? Because, they cannot see the very HOPE for the future before their eyes they were promised. They are so blinded by their unbelief that they are killing the very thing they have longed for, waited for, prayed for, for years. They have their minds made up of what their HOPE should look like, how it should arrive, when it should arrive, that when it came, in an unexpected way, they crucified their greatest gift out of fear and unbelief.

I am grateful, that Christ SAW what no one else could see. I am grateful that, while He hung there in the flesh, He SAW the world through the eyes of The Father, seeing the need for MERCY. He said, Father, forgive them for they do not know what they are doing. While we understand that God's Love was lifted on the cross, we must understand that it was MERCY that set us FREE. Give what has been given to you. It is easy to remember to love, but do not forget about the beautiful gift of the MERCY Seat.

Part IV

A NEW LIFE OF FREEDOM WITH GOD

A NEW LIFE OF FREEDOM WITH GOD

Soteriology lies within the framework of Christian Eschatology. A focus of salvation speaks to the basis for hope in a future of everlasting peace. The hope for peace, in many Christian teachings, is founded solely on the promise of entering God's Kingdom, upon dying. Though a captivating promise, unfortunately, some have taken this only literally, therefore leaving some of humanity occupied with living to die.

Teaching Christian soteriology infused with Judaism roots could affect humanity's trajectory on embracing and building the Kingdom of God by:

(1) Embracing a pluralistic view of salvation that would embody reconciliation rather than retributive justice. (2) Compelling humanity to respond to work with God in reconciling humanity, thereby bring holistic healing to relationships. Thereby giving greater meaning to the creation and life of humanity. (3) Recognizing that through the church's response to God, humanity can receive the hope promised of the blessings of God's Kingdom, on earth.

My position is not to argue the validity of heaven and hell. Neither will it stakes any claims for or against dispensationalism or end times theology. The goal is to maintain a narrow focus on the perspective of the teachings of salvation to bring purpose to the life of humanity as it relates to principles in Judaism evidenced in scripture.

Considering the conglomerate of religions that fall under the umbrella of "evangelical" religions, I will generally focus on the connection of Anabaptists, and Pentecostals (holiness). We will focus on the teachings of the Holiness religion, or movement specified in the article, *From Second Blessing to Second Coming: The Evolution of Dispensationalism within the Holiness Movement,* by Jonathan Dodrill. Within the narrative, I will provide historical content to introduce the foundation and potential challenges of this particular soteriology doctrine. This will lay the foundation to connect the doctrine to Judaism traditions and principles.

Background of the Issue

Miroslav Volf suggests that to understand how to move forward in reconciliation, we must first understand the causes of our current state. Within the narrative of this section, I will provide historical content to introduce the foundation and potential challenges of holiness soteriology doctrine. This will lay the foundation to connect the doctrine to Judaism traditions and principles.

Traditional teachings in soteriology have viewed salvation "predominately a matter of personal relationship with God that ensures ones happy existence after death."[231] Evolved terminology such as "getting to heaven" or saving souls, implies the foundation of this theology is individualist.[232] It also restricts the foundation of hope in Christianity that lies heavily in receiving it only after one dies and transcends to live eternally in God's Kingdom in heaven.

Regent College professor John Stackhouse proclaims evangelical teachings of salvation are viewed in negative terms.[233] This is substantiated in religions such as the American Ho-

---

[231] Richard Plantinga, Thomas Thompson, and Matthew Lundberg, *An Introduction to Christian Theology* (Cambridge: Cambridge University Press, 2010), 315

[232] Plantinga, Thompson and Lundberg, *An Introduction to Christian Theology,* 315

[233] Mark Kinzer, *Final Destinies: Qualifications for Receiving and Eschatological Inheritance* (Eugene: Cascade Books, 2011), 127

liness and Pentecostal Movements. The teachings are based on a three-part principle. Traditionally teachings focus on the fall of man from God through disobedience and the vital conversion or salvation. The people's salvation allows them to be set apart as chosen people.[234] Being set apart provides purpose in their role in the fulfillment of the promise of the second coming of Christ.[235] Martin Wells Knapp suggests that in this movement; Revelation was the basic story of the people living in the world waiting for Christ to bring them to heaven.[236]

While I do not pose to argue the validity of the teachings, I call to question the isolated focus of salvation. Isolating salvation to a single definition promotes the only reason for our reconciliation is to live to prepare to die. It depreciates the value and purpose of life. Greater it deprecates reasons for a reconciled life, through salvation. Humanity is called to participate in the restoration of peace and justice in the world.[237]

In a broad context, the New Testament, specifically the teachings of the Gospels, focus on the life of Christ. In the trajectory of Jesus' proclamations, he focused on the Kingdom of God "is rife with the sense of salvation as the renewed creational reign of God in which right relationships flourished between

---

[234] Jonathan Dodrill, *"From Second Blessing to Second Coming: Evolution of Dispensationalism within the Holiness Movement,"* Wesleyan Theological Journal, 2012, 159

[235] Jonathan Dodrill, *"From Second Blessing to Second Coming,",* 157

[236] Jonathan Dodrill, *"From Second Blessing to Second Coming,",* 158

[237] Marlin Miller, *"The Church in the world as the community of the Kingdom: a Radical Reformation Perspective,"* Brethern Life and Thought, 1990, 58

God, humanity and the world.[238] To understand the magnitude of his teachings, relating to salvation and humanity's right relationship with God, we must trace the teachings back to our Biblical Jewish Roots. Therefore allowing us to bridge the gap of the NT covenant highlighting the substantially meaningful purpose of the life and existence of humanity. Rather than living to die, we would die to live in the kingdom on earth as it is in heaven, as we add to the Lord's prayer in Matthew 6:9-13.

---

238 Plantinga, Thompson and Lundberg, *An Introduction to Christian Theology*, 317

Making the Connection

End time theology and saving souls have become part of a significant theological debate in western Christianity[239]. It brings the question to traditional doctrines regarding the purpose and meaning of history. More significantly, this type of apocalyptic theology focused on the soon return or "second-coming" of Christ, starting with Protestants (Anabaptists) in the sixteenth century. The promise or assurance of the second coming brought assurance to the end of suffering and persecution to the oppressed.[240] In essence, "living in the last days" also meant hope for the future. In this future, the oppressed Christians, who were faithful and following the way of Christ, would be vindicated.[241] Ironically, this future would bring an end to history.

The impending promise of impending doom to earth and new life motivated early Christians to repentance and persisted in Christian discipleship. Influenced by leaders such as Phoebe Palmer, followers were encouraged to "watch" for the second coming of Christ.[242] Through this encouragement, people were taught why salvation was vital and how to obtain it. They held strong beliefs in "sanctification" or being set apart, as this was the centrality of their doctrine.[243]

---

[239] Marlin Miller, *"The Church in the world as the community of the Kingdom,"* 52

[240] Marlin Miller, *"The Church in the world as the community of the Kingdom,"* 53

[241] Marlin Miller, *"The Church in the world as the community of the Kingdom,"* 56

[242] Jonathan Dodrill, *"From Second Blessing to Second Coming,",* 156

[243] Jonathan Dodrill, *"From Second Blessing to Second Coming,",* 151

Much like the Christians three centuries before, the "Holiness people" evolving from the Holiness movement, a break from the Protestant church, continued dispensationalist ideals. Believing, too, in the immediate need for salvation due to living in the last days, their teachings also stressed the importance of the Bible. Unlike earlier teachings, such as Wesleyan theology, which this sect broke from, Palmer emphasized that scripture was essential for salvation. This opposed Wesley's teachings that being a Christian allowed a person to believe in the Bible and the Holy Spirit being the awakener that should be responsible for sanctification.[244] The teachings of salvation through sanctification pushed a more individualist role (or individual souls) rather than previous communal restoration and justice foundations.[245] This is a demonstrative shift from "perfect love," which demands an object for God and neighbor to "saving souls" for a sanctified life (a personal state of being).[246] Furthermore, while people were encouraged to take the discipline of studying scripture, they were encouraged to do so without guidance. It was believed the Bible was not a complex, but simple book any person could easily read because it was written to be taken literally and without interpretation.[247]

Dodrill argues, Palmer's influence on salvation and dispensationalism became the framework for alternative theolo-

---

244 Jonathan Dodrill, *"From Second Blessing to Second Coming,"*, 153

245 Jonathan Dodrill, *"From Second Blessing to Second Coming,"*, 153

246 Jonathan Dodrill, *"From Second Blessing to Second Coming,"*, 154

247 Jonathan Dodrill, *"From Second Blessing to Second Coming,"*, 154

gies for the socially marginalized and lower class[248], such as liberation theology. In conjunction with the Anabaptist and Holiness principles, there is an underlying belief that Christ would come, save, reward, and take vengeance for the oppressed who followed his ways. This fuels the challenge of promoting the "new and elect people"[249] destined to live with God in the new heaven. This also questions the significance and purpose of the rest of humanity. These challenges are still present with the movement today and even creates further challenges within the movement itself, contributing to the privatization of Christianity.[250]

Redeeming Roots

Let's take a moment to examine three challenges with implications to the historical soteriology teachings within the described holiness doctrines. My goal is not to proclaim fallacies to this particular religion's doctrines or beliefs, but to propose injection of traditional Judaism to Christian teachings and why this is significant.

"There is more to salvation than saving souls."

"God invites human beings to become his partners in the work of redemption to build a society on the basis of justice that people understand as such" for in creating humanity, God gave our lives significance."[251] This would imply that sal-

---

[248] Jonathan Dodrill, *"From Second Blessing to Second Coming,"*, 160

[249] Jonathan Dodrill, *"From Second Blessing to Second Coming,"*, 161

[250] Jonathan Dodrill, *"From Second Blessing to Second Coming,"*, 161

[251] Jonathan Sacks, *To Heal A Broken World: The Ethics of Responsibility* (New York: Schocken Books, 2005), 27

vation is more than saving souls[252] and waiting for the rapture so we may die and live with God. Salvation's sole focus on souls leaves no intended purpose fo the human body, neither does placing only hope in the ultimate destruction of all humankind.

Perhaps it is easy to overlook the significance of the human body if a negative stigmatism is attached to it. Christian religion essentially concerns itself with the "brokeness" of the human body that makes one susceptible to sin.[253] Willard implies we have a body to have at our disposal the resources that would allow us to be persons in fellowship and cooperation with a personal God.[254] We have a part in our body's transformation. To live in obedience, to the Torah, as we can follow through lessons to the Israelites and from Christ, it takes a whole body, not just a soul. The body must take physical actions, therefore, has a greater purpose than leading us to sin and death.

Salvation teaching must Rejection of supersessionism

Robert Jenson argues for Christian theology of Judaism, rooted in Christology and rejecting supersessionism. The argument is The Torah reflects God's will in spite of the Jewish community's embodiment of "no" to Christ.[255] The implication here is God does not ordain supersessionism rather ordains

---

252 Mark Kinzer, *Final Destinies: Qualifications for Receiving and Eschatological Inheritance*, 126

253 Dallas Willard, *The Spirit of Disciplines: Understanding How God Changes Lives* (Broadway: Harper Collins Publishers, 1991), 30

254 Dallas Willard, *The Spirit of Disciplines*, 92

255 Michael Jay Chan, *"Reflecting on Roots: Robert Jenson's Theology of Judaism in a Pentecostal Key,"* Journal of Pentecostal Theology, 2011, 29

the existence of both communities.

Further evidence to support the idea of "existing together" is the consistent warning in both the OT and NT for humanity to not become too confident or secure in their place in God's Kingdom. Humanity should not hold any one person or group will be rewarded at the end (in judgment) while others would be punished[256] (Amos 6). Therefore, identifying the bridge of this teaching to the OT and NT could eliminate presuppositions to singling out one identity over another. The multiple references in each testament can imply the significance of the teachings for all of humanity rather than a group of people.

Futurist Hope with A New Meaning of Justice

The dispensationalism holiness teachings on salvation evolve from literal translations or interpretive readings of OT promises.[257] Taking another look at the hermeneutics of biblical literature rather than literal reading could lead to relevant insight resulting in inclusion over exclusion. A second look at salvation with the rabbinic interpretation or other outside resources or interpretations would reveal studies or views such as Dietrich Bonhoeffer and Plantinga et. al.

Dietrich Bonhoeffer would argue the exodus events of the OT, relating to the Israelites, were a form of salvation, yet this salvation could not be reduced to pertaining only to the soul.[258] While the OT speaks of individual salvation, Plantinga et al. imply the overall emphasis is the eschatological vision of a

---

[256] Mark Kinzer, *Final Destinies: Qualifications for Receiving and Eschatological Inheritance*, 129-130

[257] Michael Jay Chan, *"Reflecting on Roots"* 32

[258] Plantinga, Thompson and Lundberg, *An Introduction to Christian Theology*, 316

new heaven and earth, according to Isaiah II 1-9; 65:17-25.[259] Ultimately the idea is to consider a dualistic view of salvation that includes a reconciled life in community. Following what it means to love as written in the Torah regarding God and our relationship with others.[260]

The church, in this case, the holiness church or movement must begin to move towards a pluralistic view of salvation. Within the framework, the church would identify with past historical and canonical traditions[261] as there is a significant value within these roots. While the dispensational doctrine has motivated the holiness people towards discipleship and living in obedience with God and Christ, one must come to terms with the OT narrative and Torah teachings of Christ's ministry. Principles of salvation, extend beyond taking the name of Christ on our lips[262], or literal knowledge your bible, to receive the blessings of the Kingdom of God.

Salvation, also, pertains to the whole of human existence,[263] God redeeming the whole earth, and heading for New Jerusalem. Kinzer argues that salvation is not only about what is to come, but what is ours to enjoy and foster here and now.[264]

---

259 Plantinga, Thompson and Lundberg, *An Introduction to Christian Theology*, 316

260 Mark Kinzer, *Final Destinies: Qualifications for Receiving and Eschatological Inheritance*, 135

261 Jeffrey Lamp, "The Spirit and the Story: Some Pentecostal Musings on Robert W. Jenson's View of Scripture," Journal of Pentecostal Theology, 2011, 6

262 George Eldon Ladd, *The Gospel of the Kingdom: Scriptural Studies in The Kingdom of God* (Grand Rapids: Wm B Eerdmans Publishing Company, 1959), 96

263 Hans Schwarz, *Eschatology* (Grand Rapids: Wm B Eerdmans Publishing Company, 2000), 305

264 Mark Kinzer, *Final Destinies: Qualifications for Receiving and*

This alters the holiness terms of justice, which also frames much of liberation theology. Instead, the injection of a Judaism theology calls for changes in the trajectory of judgment and reconciliation, which are elements of the holiness teachings on salvation but from a literal, not interpretive perspective.

Bonhoeffer believes that when Christ calls a person, he bids them to come and die.[265] This implies that through our transformed life of Christian discipleship, we may transcend from our fallen state and reconnect to live again with and (unto) God. Our discipleship changes us inwardly, resurrecting us outwardly to our original positions and connecting us with God.[266] In our reincarnated life, the Kingdom of God places demands in which we must respond,[267] understanding we are no longer rulers of our own lives, we are called to embrace the work of God. In this continued work, the church must follow the Torah and teachings of Christ in lessons of redemption and reconciliation.

From the view of the oppressed or persecuted Christian, seen by holiness people, restorative justice rather than retribution justice should be the heart of its theology or dogma. After all, the concepts of redemption, which offer an offender to be redeemed, rehabilitated, and reintegrated, is at the principal of religion. These concepts, rooted in Judaism, should create an obligation, on the church, to integrate principals within its theology and put them in practice in community.[268] These

---

Eschatological Inheritance, 127

265 Dietrich Bonhoeffer, *The Cost of Discipleship* (Great Britain: SCM Press, 2001), location 138 ebook

266 Dallas Willard, *The Spirit of Disciplines*, 65

267 George Eldon Ladd, *The Gospel of the Kingdom*, 99

268 George Walters-Sleyon, *"Studies on Religion and Recidivism:*

actions open avenues of forgiveness, thereby providing solutions that promote to repair, reconciliation, and reassurance for holistic healing that involves different facets of human relationships and connections.[269]

Rather than seeking hope for a future where humanity is destroyed based on ideas of retributive dispensationalism, where only an elect people are reconciled with God, and people are predicating their lives on waiting until a new life will happen, after death, the holiness church can begin to see ways of embracing a pluralist view of salvation that can allow humanity to embrace God's Kingdom on earth. The church's role is to work with God to "save human beings"[270] or at least respond to the Kingdom to receive the kingdom.[271] This brings enlightenment to the promise of hope for better lives for humanity with God reigning in their lives.

I strongly believe that man has a responsibility to work with God in building relationships and reconciling the earth, and we are to take care of those in need, whatever that need appears to be. Two basic foundations to help with this are respect for life and how we treat our "neighbor."

Let's examine the important role of "Respect for Life" in medical care. In doing so, we will highlight challenges such as science and technology, and developing criteria for Personhood, which have altered our view of life. We will also explore a theological view to consider for providing care.

Focus on Roxbury, Dorchester, and Mattapan," Trotter Review, 2013, 37

269 George Walters-Sleyon, *"Studies on Religion and Recidivism,"* 37

270 George Walters-Sleyon, *"Studies on Religion and Recidivism,"* 45

271 George Eldon Ladd, *The Gospel of the Kingdom,* 97

Respect for life

Through work and personal experience, I have witnessed numerous complaints from individuals, suffering from illnesses, regarding how they were treated in the healthcare system. Among complaints, the greatest were: poor communication and bedside manner. Much like Teresa Maldonado describes, health care seems to have evolved into an impersonal and dehumanizing service, for some.[272]

In our effort to battle diseases like cancer, autoimmune deficiency syndrome, and any other terminal diseases have we forgotten the sanctity of life? Have we forgotten that we are to heal the individual and not just battled the disease or what it means to heal the individual?

This is a drastic change in the scope of practice for a position, where the physician was once regarded as a priest (or religious functionary).[273] Roy Branson implies that today, the challenge of medicine lies within its driven values and rituals that stand in opposition to other values.[274] Over time the advancement of science, technology, and medicine that should help to restore individuals to a life once lived, it has become a tool used to redefine the value of human life. This has shifted the focus so much on when life begins and ends, or when to start or stop care.

"No sooner have human beings mastered a new technique, the Bible seems to say that they are ready to storm the heavens and take the place of God."[275] Our role in redefining personhood reshapes our principals and predisposition toward

---

272 (Lysaught, Kotva Jr and al. 2012), 124
273 (Lysaught, Kotva Jr and al. 2012), 9
274 (Lysaught, Kotva Jr and al. 2012)
275 (Rabbi Sacks 2005), 79

life. We no longer have a "respect for life" due to life in the command of God.[276] Karl Barth wonders if we were to have a natural respect for human life would we "fully appreciate what is owed to each individual, including one's self, in his or her full solidarity and coexistence with others."[277] With the appreciation of individual life and perhaps practicing medicine as though we are treating our neighbors, this would provide a better means of administering care, therefore, making healthcare moral, personal, and theological.

Rabbi Sacks states that in Judaism, "power must always be subordinate to purpose, science to ethics, technology to human dignity. The why matters more than the how." [278] With the evolution of science and technology, unfortunately, this has not been the case in medicine. Rather than focusing on why we are given this "gift" of advanced technology, we are focused more on how to use it. We are focused on how do we save a life rather than why we are saving a life. We have shifted from how to cure a disease or ailment rather than why it is important to do so. The "how" focuses on the diagnosis or prognosis. The why allows us to draw our attention back to the life of the individual. The "why" draws us back to the "relationship of humanity."

---

276 (Lysaught, Kotva Jr and al. 2012), 721
277 (Lysaught, Kotva Jr and al. 2012), 721
278 (Rabbi Sacks 2005), 80

Personhood and Neighbors

The lawyer in the Good Samaritan Parable asks, "Who is my neighbor?" Many are unable to define their neighbor rightfully. Criteria are developed by individuals or within communities to justify whom we desire or no longer desire to have as our neighbor; whom we should help or care for and whom we should extend grace and mercy to.

Authors such as Joseph F. Fletcher imply criteria such as self-awareness, the ability to relate to others, minimal intellect, and neocortical function should be imposed, to determine personhood.[279] The criteria points back to how man quantifies the value of human life. Unfortunately, what we miss here is the danger of self-gratification filled by those imposing such value. These "so-called" values act to diminish the sanctity of human life. The new parameters require your ability to give me something to validate your existence.

Ian McFarland may argue that the theological challenge with this is Jesus (in Luke10:27) acknowledges the requirement under the law to love God and neighbor.[280] He would suggest that our need to develop criteria for personhood is designed to create"classes" of persons or beings over another.[281] The parable points out the anthropological challenges we face, even today, about class, status, division, or separation. It points out or causes us to reflect upon who to consider our neighbor and why. Those who passed by the man on the road did not help for various reasons. Whatever the reasons each passed by, they failed to "show mercy to the afflicted"[282]

---

279 (Lysaught, Kotva Jr and al. 2012), 334
280 (Lysaught, Kotva Jr and al. 2012), 373
281 (Lysaught, Kotva Jr and al. 2012), 372
282 (Lysaught, Kotva Jr and al. 2012), 374

because we are treated as persons by Christ and called to related to others as such.

Oliver O'Donovan suggests that "we discover the personhood of the other by his dealings with us."[283] First, we must understand that persons and neighbors are interchangeable terms. Rather than creating criteria for persons, we must realize that "the term person is clearly intended to be a universal term, in the way neighbour is" as pointed out by Jesus in the parable. O'Donovan describes three responsibilities to our a neighbor. We should actively engage with him and care for him. We should sympathize with him. Finally, we are to protect him. Through engagement, we prove to be a neighbor in our commitment rather than dependent upon the value of the other person's social contribution.[284]

As we continue to view the imposed criteria of what determines a person, we use these parameters to decide whom to care for and how, as it relates to.[285] The challenge is we are using the same intrinsic value system to determine who is worth caring for. Persons are understood to have a right to a certain level or quality of treatment that would rule out, making them treated as objects.[286]

It is believed this criterion is required to differentiate between how to treat an inanimate object versus a person that should have certain inalienable rights. However, if we consider the views of authors such as McFarland and O'Donovan, viewing neighbors as persons, does this view change when one becomes sick? Do they become less of a person? Fletcher's views

---

283 (Lysaught, Kotva Jr and al. 2012), 367
284 (Lysaught, Kotva Jr and al. 2012), 367
285 (Lysaught, Kotva Jr and al. 2012), 377
286 (Lysaught, Kotva Jr and al. 2012), 373

would suggest so. Stanley Hauerwas suggests the "language of person seems convenient to use, however, because we wish to assume that our medicine still rests on a consensus of moral beliefs."[287] It is implied that using the language of "person" allows us to escape the moral responsibility to provide care for others, after all, how often do we refer to ourselves as "person"? Hauerwas states how often he identifies himself as "Stanley Hauerwas, teacher, husband, father or ultimately a Texan"[288] nor does he refer to others as persons. The implication is individuals are unique and have unique needs.

Patients as Neighbors

The authors discuss various medical challenges in their view of developing personhood criteria. Here we will examine some of their examples using applying the concept of treating patients as neighbors versus persons.

O'Donovan discusses the difficult decision to withdraw care for someone in an irreversible coma is a patient or not. He implies we know the patient is still a human, yet the question one should consider is, or criteria used should be if the "he is no longer he."[289] Through our engagement, this brotherly loyalty is owed. The measures he uses also aligns with aspects of Hauerwas views, seeing the human as an individual. Furthermore, we are enacting McFarland's view of providing love and care for the neighbor. These combined views are contrary to Fletcher, who would consider a categorized persons approach, determining the value to the individual. Though the goal of developing criteria is to prevent treating patients like objects, unfortunately, when we begin to

---

287 (Lysaught, Kotva Jr and al. 2012), 379
288 (Lysaught, Kotva Jr and al. 2012), 378
289 (Lysaught, Kotva Jr and al. 2012), 368

formulate checklists and to assign value based on self-imposed ideas, we, in fact, begin to do the opposite of our intent. Fletcher's view would cause us to first change who or what this individual is by placing a new definition to them man as created.

If we applied the rationale of treating a patient as our neighbor, then we may return to focusing on individual needs and not just fighting to cure a disease. William May implies that an element of the physician's oath is his promise to fulfill his duties to his patient.[290] For those who have challenges viewing practicing medicine from a theological perspective, the oath still carries a philanthropic ideal of service to humankind. While a physician may not cure a patient, he may still "heal in the sense of helping to keep the patient while in the face of ineliminable adversity."[291] To do this, a relationship must exist. The physician must engage with the patient to understand the identity of the individual thereby able to conclude what "wholeness" means for the individual. Anything contrary would cause the physician to become fixated on "checklists" of symptoms of suffering. The challenge with blanket checklists is that suffering varies from patient to patient just as the same treatment does not always work for the same diagnosis. The more enhanced our interactions within the framework of relationships, perhaps the more we can refocus on the "why" or purpose of medicine rather than the how. Perhaps, then we will have a greater "Respect for Life" rather than finding reasons to redefine who is a person and who is not.

I was led to interview Deandrea Myrick, a 33-year-old author residing in New Jersey, who was diagnosed with Cerebral

---

290 (Lysaught, Kotva Jr and al. 2012), 235
291 (Lysaught, Kotva Jr and al. 2012), 242

Palsy, as a very young age. Her story was somewhat familiar to me as I was fortunate enough to witness aspects of her journey and transformation in her condition.

Cerebral Palsy is a syndrome that impairs the central nervous system and the development of gross motor function. It occurs in every 2/1000 to 2.5/1000 live births. Most are diagnosed sometime during infancy and preschool after showing one or more signs of "abnormal reflexes, floppiness or rigidity of the limbs and trunk, abnormal posture, involuntary movements, or unsteady walking..."[292]

Most of Deandrea's memories began with the challenges of attempting to adjust or fit in at school, with her condition. She recalls spending much of her childhood plagued by necessary and unnecessary medical appointments, tests, and studies. In addition to the many decisions made on her behalf to make her life better, some were made that also caused her scars from moments of embarrassment as she was forced to stand out more than she cared to. Already carrying the weight of her disability that caused her to stand out in school, she tried to do whatever she could to avert additional attention yet, sometimes it was unavoidable.

In her youth, to help provide support to her weakened limbs, she wore, what she describes as heavy and painful braces. To correct motor function and vision, she had surgery on her eye and was required to wear an eye patch. She understands these were necessary, but she struggled with what she considered unnecessary decisions. She shared a memory of entering a new year of school, only to find her parents and teachers decided she would benefit from having a larger and specialized desk. This equipment was to help her become

---

292 (Mayo Clinic Staff n.d.)

more organized as she recalls teachers comparing her lack of organizational skills to another student. Unfortunately, she felt picked on as she also noticed plenty of students, without disabilities, whose desks were "messier than mine. Why did I require a desk that made me stand out?" She felt no one would listen to her, including her mother. Everyone blamed the need on her medical condition. She believes she could have been afforded additional assistance, after all, the desk proved to only make matters worse in the end.

She describes an accident she encountered when she tripped and fell off the school bus. The reaction from her mother, she believes was extreme. She was no longer allowed to ride the regular bus with students. She was now required to ride a special bus with specialized assistance, again drawing unjustified attention to her disability. The incident and decision were yet, another example of lack of listening and support from her immediate community.

The same treatment would continue throughout her life as she encountered other teachers, students, and even health professionals. She felt people would rudely stare at her. Teachers would question why she walked "so slow or lazy," and she was forced to continually defend herself. To some degree, this made her initially defensive and closed off. Interestingly enough, she notes that while attending a Christian school, she received the greatest support from teachers and staff, yet made the least friendships with other students. Here is where she was ridiculed the most by fellow students. In public school, she was harassed more by teachers and at least spoken to, more, by fellow students.

She did not start attending church (on a semi-regular basis) until she was in high school. You would think she would have received more support, yet it seemed it was more pity support than anything else. Met often with empathetic greetings, reflecting "poor helpless DD" she felt she was not supported here either. Even during a major operation that should have corrected her feet, yet made it worse, there was indeed a lack of support. As she has gotten older, with the continued limitations and significant restrictions placed upon her from her overall community, her condition continued to decline. Her levels of pain only increased almost debilitating her. She could neither stand, walk, nor sit for prolonged periods. Trips to the store would require a motorized scooter, for mobility. She also needed assistance just to step up and off a curb.

With each visit to a physician, she explains she felt the doctors were not listening to her or understanding how much she was suffering. She was given more and more pain pills and told there was nothing anyone could do besides offer physical therapy and painkillers. She was told this would be her life. As a Christian, she was conflicted and kept praying that God would somehow heal her body and relieve the pain. She began to explain how she resorted to different sources for answers, even following Benny Hinn, hoping God would hear and answer her somehow. Deandrea just wanted the suffering to stop, and those around her were not listening. She did not want to be on pain medication, and injections for the rest of her life believed there had to be another answer.

In the last two years, her life has changed drastically. She has been able to do things she was told she would never be able to accomplish. She no longer requires bulky special orthotics, though she uses small inserts in her sneakers. She proudly wears "cute" name brand sneakers and shoes that she was once told she would never wear. She has a new community of doctors, who also happen to be younger and closer to her age. She believes this makes a difference in her care as they tend to listen to her. Once required to utilize a motorized scooter, she is now able to walk for long periods and jog very slowly. I recall the first time she ran and her first 3-mile walk with no pain. It was an emotional and exciting time. She has made changes to her community, to include her church, where she has tremendous support. No longer does she stand out for her disability, but she is recognized as a whole person and neighbor. She has a new circle of friends, yet she still struggles with her certain aspects of her family. Even with the transformation and new found independence, her immediate family has lost sight of their "identity." Once the primary caregivers, now no longer needed in that capacity, they too often still attempt to instill limitations on Deandrea only so she would be required to depend upon them. Unfortunately, this has caused a rift in some aspects of their relationships.

Oliver O'Donovan discusses Jesus' Good Samaritan parable and points out Jesus's message. We are shown" how we identify our neighbor; from our active engagement with him in caring for him, sympathizing with him, protecting him."[293] As much as we discover who our neighbor is, the Gentile in the story discovers the identity of his neighbor. Reflecting on Deandra's story, it is interesting that she does not truly discover her neighbors until age 32 as she begins to find her identity in a separate community from her immediate family. Though she received help from her family throughout the years, the support received made her less empowered and more confined and restricted. Before this transformation treated much like a disabled child, her relationships portrayed Stanley Hauerwas' explanation of Michael Tooley's personhood theory. Here children, more specifically infants, are not persons and therefore do not bear rights necessary

---

293 (Lysaught, Kotva Jr and al. 2012), 367

to make infanticide a morally questionable practice. Medical care is provided on their behalf strictly from the motive of charity.[294] Perhaps the greater stance is that as a neighbor, we have a perceive expectation of " a give and take societal relationship." If one is unable to participate in the giving aspect reasonably, then it makes it difficult for others to give. Seeing one with a disability, such as hers, although her CP is quite mild, she was looked upon as one who could not equally contribute to others, therefore often excluded. To those within her family, somehow they felt the same; consequently, they overprotected her, over-celebrated accomplishments, and limited her ability to make personal and medical decisions.

Spending time researching her condition, for herself, and spending time talking with experts independently, she has gained the confidence to participate actively in her medical care and control her relationships with medical professionals. In fact, she now requires less medical care and attention. Mary Anne Warren and Fletcher suggests personhood "exists in the possession cluster of five traits: consciousness, reasoning, self-motivated activity, the capacity to communicate, and the presence of self-concepts and self-awareness."[295]. Though her immediate family struggles in disagreement, Deandrea no doubt fits Warren and Fletcher's definition of personhood. It is with these traits, she has readjusted with her medical condition.

As she described her battles with suffering, I am reminded of McKenny's discussion of Plato's question of moral suffering. "What limits should we observe in our efforts to im-

---

294 (Lysaught, Kotva Jr and al. 2012), 378
295 (Lysaught, Kotva Jr and al. 2012), 389

prove bodily performance and remove causes of suffering?"[296] Plagued by agonizing pain, this young lady would cry to God, wondering why He has not healed her. Understanding the limitations of a doctor, based on her Christian beliefs, her belief aligns with Sulmasy's covenant theory. Sulmasy explains the deuterocanonical text of Ben Sira as it pertains to the covenant relationship between God, doctor, and patient. The relationship is a covenant trust between doctor and patient authorized by the orientation of the covenant to the overarching covenant between God and all of God's people.[297] Therefore, in her case, God would, through her faith and her doctors, heal her body from suffering agonizing pain. Following the changes, she ultimately made in her life, and though those were her beliefs, perhaps the covenant did not exist in the initial relationships. After all, those were not the physicians with whom she built a relationship. Those relationships were all built with those who initially controlled her medical care and excluded her from decisions. This conclusion may seem far-fetched, but when we examine the holistic approach to her care, as well as dos Anjos, described levels of doing bioethics, it may be possible.

Dos Anjos describes the microsocial level as extending principally to interpersonal relationships that involve the doctor, the sick person, and his or her family.[298] From birth to age 31, this was the relationship of care for Deandrea. Though she was the second party in this relationship, she was excluded from discussions even while present in exam rooms. Even as a capable adult, oft times her mother and doctor would talk over or around her. When she attempted to ask them not to,

---

[296] (Lysaught, Kotva Jr and al. 2012), 398
[297] (Lysaught, Kotva Jr and al. 2012), 307
[298] (Lysaught, Kotva Jr and al. 2012), 89

her mother would take offense, promise not to do it again, yet become a repeat offender. Everyone would tell her what to do about her care rather than listen to her needs and desires. These events added to her periods of suffering.

John D. Roth implies that as social beings, we have a natural expectation for the community to assist us in our ability to live, flourish, and participate in the life of our society.[299] Based on Deandrea's interview, her expectations were initially unmet until she became a member of a new community, apart from her immediate family. This community now comprised of separate medical, social, and church support systems have now begun to meet that expectation. She also has been able to thrive by helping others to do the same. Once the child that just wanted to fit in and be accepted as normal or like everyone else has now found her place to do so. Her transformation has been holistic.

---

299 (Lysaught, Kotva Jr and al. 2012), 135

As a woman of color who has experienced and overcome her share of adversity, I feel it is important to speak up, sharing my life with the hopes it will encourage and empower.

Too often we walk through life, witnessing or experiencing, sometimes, traumatic situations, yet find ourselves impacted in ways that leave us malfunctioning. We find ourselves unable to properly handle relationships, unable to use the best wisdom in making decisions, in unhealthy and unwarranted situations, and unable to realize our self-worth.

Recently, I had the opportunity and privilege of being a guest on Advance Your Art podcast, hosted by Yuri Cataldo. During the interview, we discussed parts of my journey through life, such as my time in the Air Force and what influenced my decisions to not only enlist but to stay and serve for 20 years. We also discussed my experience as an author, to include the inspiration for each published book, along with quite a few other subjects. It was quite an interesting interview, thanks to Yuri, as he has a way of interacting with guests to draw out their stories. The interview aired on Thursday, 10 January. What I found very interesting and kept me thinking long after our recording was Yuri's final question. What was the best advice I've received? My response, "To know your worth." It was loaded advice that came through a simple message, but it has stuck with me over the years. It has also continued to take on a deeper meaning and understanding as I continue to move forward living my life in purpose and on purpose.

Since the interview, I have further reflected on this advice in light of so much that is in the news lately, especially seeing people in "powerful positions" take advantage of others, the debates between people over who is at fault when people are taken advantage of, or listening to how easy people come up with "answers" to problems by condemning and shaming others.

Recently, I listened to and read many comments regarding the infamous and trending series about R Kelly. I saw everything from being shocked about his abuse (which was neither a secret or new news, mind you), to people expressing concerns about the victims and survivors, but not without condemning the parents of the victims. Some people took the path of elevating themselves to condemn these parents, who continue to suffer, by explaining how much they hover over their children, implying this was the "answer" to the problem. What I found even more interesting were less than unsympathetic comments towards the victims and survivors. Instead, several people still sided with the victimizer, also feeling the need to express support by focusing on "how people were trying to take his money."

Now, I am a pretty level headed person. That means I do not get drawn into things based on emotions. I know people were more disgusted by the actions of the victimizer, but honestly, from what I have witnessed, those high emotions caused them to do what exactly…vent on social media…ok, now what?

I say this because this is the same person these same people listened to and supported for decades while ALL of his actions were in the news and on the radio. Even years ago, when certain incidents became public, people became "disgusted" and outraged. They complained and talked about it until it died down and something else came along. Meanwhile, they went back to supporting the "artist" and whatever he did. The problem is deeper than the issue of complaining and moving on. The problem is that as a community, as a people, overall, we have either lost sight of or never really understood our

WORTH. We become easily vulnerable and easily comprised as a result of not knowing what we are worth.

When we live in a world or society where people will hurt or kill one another over material things, it means we fail to understand our worth. When we are willing to spend time with anyone to get what we think we need or want, we fail to understand our worth. When we believe that enslaving ourselves to a system that will work us until our dying breath just to have material things, we fail to understand our worth. When we are willing to accept anything because we believe that is the only way to get your foot in the door, then we fail to understand our worth. When we try to paint a pretty public life to gain acceptance or fit in with others, we fail to understand our worth. Even how we deal with and see others reflect how we understand our worth. When you take situations like those further exposed by this T.V. documentary, and the comments of those speaking against the victims and survivors, accusing them of still desiring fame and money, it speaks to the heart of how we value ourselves.

A person who cannot objectively listen to the stories, but would rather condemn, believing this is about money, I would argue, reflects aspects of the victimizer they are learning more about. In those moments, they value the power, fame, popularity, glorification, money, celebrity status more than life itself. To them, those things signify life rather than having life, and using those things received wisely and responsibly. The result of what we have or can obtain somehow becomes our life and determines or perceived worth. Either we have never learned or forgot along the way who we are and that our life is (or should be) sacred and is of great value.

As a child of The King, I am worth more than money and riches can buy. As a child of The King, I am not or will ever be a slave to anything. Rather, as I am a child of God, I am FREE to LIVE a life that pays me. A long time ago, a life was freely given for me. This life paid the ultimate price for me so that I may become a child of The Most High and an heir to His kingdom. I have rights to all that He owns, thus no need to sell my self to whatever comes my way. I take stock in knowing this, therefore understanding that I must be mindful in the decisions I make and the actions I take regarding my life. This is a must for I desire not to allow myself to depreciate but to gain interest during my life. I wish to increase, not decrease.

Because I understand my worth, I am mindful of where I invest my time and energy; therefore, I take stock in the company I keep and the actions I take. I want and keep people around who will be honest and provide constructive criticism. Not those who continuously hang on to my every word, just to fill my inflate head with "air" - the useless, unsubstantiated remarks that just boost my ego. If my head is filled with hot air, resulting in an oversaturated ego. Where does that get me? Perhaps like those we see, in power, surrounded by others, I call flunkies who are willing to keep the powerful pleased, despite the cost. Actions are taken even if that means compromising themselves and anyone else, they are in contact with, including me.

In our society, we teach people they "must play along to get along," which I believe can be quite dangerous. Just how far should someone "play along to "get along?" Should they compromise their morals and values just to get what they ultimately desire? Should they stoop down and play along as if they are less than, just to boost up someone else as a means to get what they want? What type of expectations and standard are we setting or allowing people to set for themselves by encouraging them to "play along to get along?" Are we not past the days of making people "shuck and jive" just to make "boss" happy? Have we not evolved or learned anything?

I want to keep people around and ensure I do things that will help me increase my value rather than allow me to depreciate. Becoming less valuable not only to myself but to those I may impact or influence along my journey. I have no desire to forfeit my freedom, becoming a slave to people and things of this world, when I am already an heir to The Kingdom. Why would I desire to trade my position as an heir for that of a slave? Why become less than when I am a child I God, am already more than and the longer I stay with Him, I am guaranteed the greatest return on investment.

It is crucial that we deal with issues such as how we raise our children, influencing how they see not just us, but also themselves. Even in demonstration, through our actions, how we live our lives, we allow them to see the value of knowing their worth. Who we spend our time with, how we spend our time, these are not simply actions but actions of investments. The things we spend time discussing, debating, arguing about demonstrates not only what we value, but speaks to how we value our self. It speaks to what we believe is worth the investment of our time. Therefore, senseless debates that result in no action may perhaps be a waste of time spent, especially if nothing in that debate was "healthy," but rather overheated emotions toiling back and forth with neither side never listening to nor hearing the other.

What always troubles my mind, even more, is listening to and watching those who claim to follow God...believe in Christ, that fall into all of these situations.

How can people who believe they were created in the image and likeness of The Creator, fail to see or understand their worth? Perhaps it is a result of who has our ear and what we worship. Perhaps it is a result of creating or following other gods, therefore taken on the grave image of those idols. Our idols can be fame, fortune, acceptance, popularity, exaltation, prestige, money, cars, clothes, and even how we define or determine success.

The chase, of such idols, makes us vulnerable to areas of danger that can become cancerous to our life. The chase of idols takes us far from where we need to be killing our identity and depreciating our value. At the sake of missing out or losing an idol, we "sell out." We sell ourselves to the lowest bidder yet, at the highest price. It's time to take stock in who we are to whom we belong. Take stock in how we define power and success…take stock in how we define wealth and riches…take stock in what is driving or guiding us…take stock in understanding and knowing our worth.

If you have begun to trade your freedom for enslavement, there is still HOPE. Remember, all cannot be lost because the ultimate…the greatest price for you was paid long ago. The key is your willingness…your desire to regain your rightful place. The perception of yourself must begin to change… seeing yourself through the eyes of The One who paid it all for you, rather than what you have given yourself to. Turn away from what you idolize and give your heart to The One who has already SAVED you. The only thing that can hold you from your destiny is truly YOU.

Know Your Worth. Realize your value, if necessary, return to your place as Children of God, heirs to The Kingdom and Never Compromise who you know you are.

Some of the greatest people who made the greatest impact in this world were misunderstood and unrecognizable to the average person. Just because those who met and encountered them could not recognize them, could not understand them, this did not negate who they were. Their identity did not change. Their gifts did not change. What they would bring to this earth to leave a forever lasting impression, would not change.

Pablo Picasso was a great artist. While his family saw some of this work, the minimized his gifts and talents. They could not see the great potential of his gift, therefore "defining" how his gift should be used. The same can be said for many of his would-be teachers. They had an idea of what art should be or should look like. They could not see the art Picasso was creating as it was "unusual" and different. For this, they called it wrong and "corrected" him. Considered "rebellious" and a bad student, he was "punished" for defying instruction, ultimately leaving the school and traditional training. Today, a hand-drawn, hand signed numbered sketch could cost you $20K. His paintings could cost $100K or over $200K. All for work from someone that was once kicked

Look at the years it took Steve Jobs to establish his brand. Most could not wrap their minds around what he was creating because it was unusual and abnormal. Even Jesus was misunderstood and unrecognizable for who he was and established on this earth to do. Unrecognizable to those in his own town, who only saw him as the son of Joseph and not the Son of God.

We become so familiar with people in their natural state that we fail to see them through the eyes of God. Our vision is impaired, seeing what we want, therefore keeping that individual "trapped" in our defined image. Think for a minute. The little child we see running around playing with their "toys," years later, we still see them as little so and so. Forever in our minds, that is all of who they are, therefore, as they have grown to accomplish great things or are growing to accomplish great things, we fail to see it. Instead, we pick on them, we diminish the work they have accomplished, we think, it is just "cute."

Too often, the opposite happens and what that person is working to accomplish is completely ignored and pushed aside while the individual is mocked and ridiculed. But today, I want to encourage those who have been "trapped" behind the labels and stigmas of the blind. Yes, the blind. These people are blind because their vision is impaired, not yours. When we have difficulty seeing what is inside of an individual, who an individual is or becoming, it has much to do with how we SEE God.

For years, the people always anticipated the arrival of the king, the Savior that would come and redeem them. But when the day came, even after what was written, that "the virgin shall conceive and bear a son and they shall name him Emmanuel, which means God is with us" they still could neither see nor accept that this was what they Hoped for. Why? Because we have defined God, therefore defining how He moves, how He operates, how He creates, how He designs. Our world and the world around us is in the image in which we create, therefore, so are those we see on a given day. Our impaired vision is so obscured that we fail to see that someone or something bears the nature and the giftings of the Lord and our Savior.

We give labels to define people based on what we see from an earthly vision rather than from a heavenly vision. This earthly vision traps, creates barriers, hinders, creates obstacles, and attempts to close doors. But, to those who have been living behind the stigmas and labels of the blind. Those have been fighting the unnecessary obstacles placed before them, thanks to the vision impaired. Those who were hindered because of the "disability" of others. Those who were ignored, pushed aside, ridiculed, and mocked because of what God put in you. Know that YOU ARE WHO YOU ARE. Nothing has changed simply because others around you could not see. Remember, if they could not see God, then how could they see you.

If they could only see God as a giver based on what they needed at the moment, as if He was someone we make a wish upon rather than the Provider of our all of our needs, all of the time, even before we saw our needs, then how would you expect them to see you.

If they could only see God when their days were good, yet could not see Him during the tough times, failing to recognize Him as The ONE who gives us the strength to endure all things, all of the time, then how could you expect them to SEE you. If they could only see GOD as one who gives from time to time, rather than The Creator who governs all things, then how could they see you. These are the same ones who believe they must walk through life "figuring things out" and trying to make a way for things to happen, all while struggling with their Peace. Yet, you, the "ridiculed" knew that this is and was never the way of God. For, if he is the Creator of all things, and have established us all in the earth, then would He just place you here idly, without a plan or purpose for your life?

If we read sixty-six books in the Bible, how have we come away believing that God works or moves without purpose? How can we read Sixty-six books in the Bible, failing to SEE that God always moved in what we now consider unusual ways and did what we consider abnormal things? The key words are "what we consider unusual, what we consider abnormal." The fact is, people reject what they do not understand and create labels to help people and things fit their understanding. But just as those who have gone before you. Those would walk in a similar path, the righteous shall always be redeemed.

To the misunderstood...stay true to who you are. Stay true to creating the unexplainable, the unimaginable, the incomprehensible because this is who God created you to be. See, it is those who stand out. Those who God have given this nature to, those He has placed His hand on to replicate this nature in the earth...the nature to CREATE...keep CREATING. Keep pressing into what God has placed in your heart.

He has impressed into your heart something great that will impact this earth and as just as He placed it there, nothing or no one will be able to shut it down...well, except you. If what is in your heart does not come forth from you, it is because you have given way to the blind rather than walking in the light of Christ. The light of Christ will continue to lead you to SEE the Father and his plans for you.

So never allow yourself to get trapped behind the obstacles of the vision impaired people, for the Lord is a WAY MAKER... you will overcome any and all things before you. He will show you the way to go, the way to move, the way to walk with Him to get to the place He created for you.

Nothing can stop God's plans for He is the creator and governing authority of this earth, of this world. All power, all authority belongs to God and no one but Him. You just have to decide if you will give way to the powerless (people) or the POWERFUL ONE.

He created you, not the people. They can only hinder how you SEE God if you allow them to put blinders on you. Share not their darkness. Share not their blindfolds. Share not in their skepticism. Share not their misunderstandings. Share not their limited mindset.

Do not assimilate with the land inhabitants and you will not lose your identity. When you stay true to who God said you are and what he called you to do, YHWH will retain his covenant with you.

You can change the world when you walk with God, allowing Him to keep your eyes open and set on Him. You want HOPE for the future? Stay active in the ways of God. What he has given you to create. He has given you the keys to change the future, and those who are stuck in the past will never see you for who God created you to be and created to do. This does not change you who are!

Show them how to SEE God in your life as you continue to keep your sights on him while he breaks every barrier, every obstacle, and every stronghold. While it seems, they are hating...God is also using you to change their perspective of HOPE for the future. Perhaps more than you expect will catch on. Perhaps more than you realize will begin to see. Perhaps more than you realize will drop their blindfolds, or the scales will fall off of their eyes, so they will too SEE GOD as HE works through you.

Never downplay your gifts, talents, or skills to fit in!

You will continue in life to meet people who will never recognize or acknowledge who you are or are meant to be. It is important that when you encounter these people, you do not allow yourself to become something that you are not, simply because they cannot see who God says you are.

Remember "it is written, 'What no eye has seen, nor ear heard, nor the heart of man imagined, what God has prepared for those who love him'— these things God has revealed to us through the Spirit." Many are just not ready for you. Not ready for what God is doing in your life but stay faithful and He will move you into places that even you would never expect. Trust in His plans for you, even when you do not understand them. You may feel left out or that you must stand alone, but you are never alone. God just wants you to learn to rely upon Him more than you do humans. He desires to open your eyes to the true identity He has created for you. He desires to open your mind and heart to the endless possibilities you have when you are walking with Him. He will show you where He has made room for you to do great things.

So, trust Him and His word for your life even when others cannot see or fail to believe. The truth is, they are not rejecting you, their problem is with God. We must learn to live by the Spirit rather than the flesh. Living by the Spirit allows us to gain insight and wisdom to things we would not and could not comprehend when living by the flesh.

Stay FREE, never bound, and losing yourself in the confines of the limited minds of man. Rather live in the endless possibilities with God. Be Free to whom God has called you to be! He will not fail you.

References

Aland, Kurt. 1968. "The Relation Between Church and State In Early Times: A Reinterpretation." *The Journal of Theological Studies, New Series* 19 (1): 115-27. Accessed 2018. http://www.jstor.org.fuller.idm.oclc.org/stable/23959560.

Allen , Holly Catterton, and Christine Lawton Ross. 2012. *Intergenerational Christian Formation: Bringing the Whole Church Together in MInistry, Community and Worship.* Downers Grove, IL: InterVarsity Press.

Alter, Robert. 2013. *Ancient Israel: The Former Prophets: Joshua, Judges, Samuel, And Kings.* New York: W.W. Norton & Company.

Anderson, Bernhard W. 1957. "The Place of Shechem in the Bible." *The Biblical Archaeologist* (The American Schools of Oriental Research) 20 (1): 10-19. Accessed August 2018. doi:10.2307/3209167.

Anderson, Ray S. 2001. *The Shape of Practical Theology: Empowering Ministry with Theological Praxis.* Downers Grove: InterVarsity Press.

Bantum, Brian. 2016. "The Death of Race: Building a New Christianity in a Racial World." (Augsburg Fortress, Publishers). http://www.jstor.org.fuller.idm.oclc.org/stable/j.ctt1c84g1t.

Benjamin, Daniel J, James J Choi, and A. Joshua Strickland. 2010. "Social Identity and Preferences." *American Economic Association* (American Economic Association) 100 (4): 1913-1928. http://www.jstor.org.fuller.idm.oclc.org/stable/27871281.

Benner, PhD, David G. 2011. *Soulful Spirituality: Becoming Fully Alive and Deeply Human.* Grand Rapids: BrazosPress.

Bolsinger, Tod E. 2004. *It Takes a Church to Raise a Christian: How the Community of God Transforms Lives.* Grand Rapids, Michigan: Brazos Press.

Bonhoeffer, Dietrich. 2001. *The Cost of Discipleship.* Great Brittain: SCM Press.

Buxton, Graham. 2016. *Dancing In The Dark: The Privilege of Participating in God's Ministry in the World.* Eugene, Oregon: Cascade Books.

Castelo, Daniel. 2012. "Holiness Simpliciter: A Wesleyan Engagement and Proposal In Light of John Webster's Trinitarian Dogmatics of Holiness." *Wesleyan Theological Journal* 47 (2): 147-164. Accessed June 2018. ATLA Religion Database with ATLASerials PLUS, EBSCOhost.

Cavanaugh, William T. 2008. *Being Consumed.* Grand Rapids, Michigan: William B, Eerdmans Publishing Company.

Chadwick, Henry. 1993. *The Early Church.* London: The Penguin Group.

Chan, Michael Jay. 2011. "Reflecting on Roots: Robert Jenson's Theology of Judaism in a Pentecostal Key." *Journal of Pentecostal Theology* 20 (1): 27-37. Accessed May 2018. doi:Academic Search Premier, EBSCOhost.

Chung, Youn Ho. 2010. *The Sin of the Calf: The Rise of the Bibles Negative Attitude Toward the Golden Calf.* New York: T&T Clark; eBook Academic Collection (EBSCO Host).

De Ste, Croix, G. E. M. . 1954. "Aspects of the "Great" Persecution." *The Harvard Theological Review* 47 (2): 75-113. http://www.jstor.org.fuller.idm.oclc.org/stable/1508458.

DeGroat, Chuck. 2014. *toughest people to love: how to understand, lead, and love the difficult people in your life - including yourself.* Grand Rapids, Michigan: William B. Eerdmans Publishing Company.

Dodrill, Jonathan. 2012. "From Second Blessing to Second Coming: The Evolution of Dispensationalism within the Holiness Movement." *Wesleyan Theological Journal* 47 (1): 150-161. Accessed May 2018. ATLA Religion Database with ATLASerials PLUS, EBSCOhost.

n.d. *Early Church: Persuctions in the Early Church.* Accessed October 2018. https://www.earlychurch.org.uk/persecution.php.

Ehler, Sidney, and John Morral, . 1954. *Church and state throught the centuries: a collection of historic documents with commentaries.* London: Burns & Oats.

Eusebius. 2005. *Ecclesiastical History, (books 6-10).* Vol. 29, in *The Fathers of the Church: A New Translation*, by Roy J Defarrari. Washington, DC: Catholic University of America Press.

Eusebius. 1999. "Life of Constatine." In *Claredon Ancient History Series*, by Averil Cameron and Stuart Geroge. Oxford: Oxford University Press. https://search-ebscohost-com.fuller.idm.oclc.org/login.aspx?direct=true&db=e000xna&AN=155692&site=ehost-live.

Gillespie, Jennifer Z, Patrick D Converse, and S. David Kriska. 2010. "Applying Recommendations from the LIterature on Stereotype Threat: Two Field Studies." *Journal of Business and Psychology* (Springer) 25 (3): 493-504. http://www.jstor.org.fuller.idm.oclc.org/stable/40682668.

Gonzalez, Justo L. 2010. *The Story of Christianity.* Second. New York, New York: HarperCollins.

Green, Joel B. 2007. *Seized By Truth: Reading The Bible As Scripture.* Nashville, Tennessee: Abingdon Press.

Gunton, Colin E. 1997. *The Promise of Trinitarian Theology.* Edinburgh: T&T Clark.

Heifetz, Ronald A., and Marty Linsky. 2002. *Leadership On The Line: Staying Alive through the Dangers of Leading.* Boston: Harvard Business School Press.

Hooper, Michael. 1976. "The Structure and Measurement of Social Identity." *The Public Opinion Quarterly* (Oxford University Press on behalf of the American Association for Public Opinion Research) 40 (2): 154-164. http://www.jstor.org.fuller.idm.oclc.org/stable/2748201.

Ignatius, Polycarp, and William Reeves. 1889. *The Epistles of St. Ignatius and St. Polycarp.* Accessed October 2018. https://search-ebscohost-com.fuller.idm.oclc.org/login.aspx?direct=true&db=h7h&AN=36811147&site=ehost-live.

Irwin, Brian P. 2012. "Not Just Any King: Abimelech, the Northern Monarchy, and the Final Judges." *Journal of Biblical LIterature* (The Society of Biblical Literature) 131 (3): 443-454. Accessed August 2018. doi:10.2307/23488248.

2017. *Jane Elliott.* Accessed December 2018. http://janeelliott.com.

Jennings, Willie James. 2017. *Acts: Belief A Theological Commentary on the Bible.* Edited by Amy Plantinga Pauw and William C Placher. Louisville, Kentucky: Wesminster John Knox Press.

Johnson, David, and Van Vonderen. 1991. *The Subtle Power of Spiritual Abuse: Recognizing & Escaping Spiritual Manipulation and False Spiritual Authority Within The Church.* Minneapolis, Minnesota: Bethany House Publishers.

Kinnaman, David. 2011. *You Lost Me: Why Young Christians Are Leaving The Church...And Rethinking Faith.* Grand Rapids, Michigan: BakerBooks.

Kinnaman, David, and Gabe Lyons. 2007. *Unchristian: What A New Generation Really Thinks About Christianity.* Grand Rapids, Michigan: Baker Books.

Klingshirn, William E, and Linda Safran. 2007. *The Early Christian Book (CUA Studies in Early Christianity).* Washington, DC: Catholic University of America Press. https://search-ebscohost-com.fuller.idm.oclc.org/login.aspx?direct=true&db=e000xna&AN=493610&site=ehost-live.

Lactantius, L.C.F., and Gilbert Barnet. 1687. *A relation of the death of the primitive persecutors.* Amsterdam. Accessed November 2018.

Ladd, George Eldon. 1959. *The Gospel of the Kingdom: Scriptural Studies in The Kingdom of God.* Grand Rapids: Wm. B. Eerdmans Publishing Company.

Lamp, Jeffrey S. 2011. "The Spirit and the Story: Some Pentecostal Musings on Robert W. Jenson's View of Scripture." *Journal of Pentecostal Theology* 20 (1): 5-14. Accessed June 2018. Academic Search Premier, EBSCOhost.

Lartey, Emmanuel Y. 2006. *Pastoral Theology in an Intercultural World.* Eugene, Oregon: WIPF & STOCK.

Lysaught, M. Therese, Joseph Kotva Jr, and et al. 2012. *On Moral Medicine Theological Perspectives in Medical Ethics.* Third Edition. Grand Rapids, Michigan: William B. Eermans Publishing Company.

Mahaffy, Samuel. 2014. *Appreciative Inquiry for Faith-Based Organizations.* Feb 5. https://youtu.be/uUufArT0h8Y.

Mason, Arthur James. 1876. *The Persecution of Diocletian: A Historical Essay.* Deighton Bell and Co. Accessed Oct 2018. https://search-ebscohost-com.fuller.idm.oclc.org/login.aspx?direct=true&db=h7h&AN=36332973&site=ehost-live.

Mayo Clinic Staff. n.d. *Mayo Clinic Foundation.* https://www.mayoclinic.org/diseases-conditions/cerebral-palsy/symptoms-causes/syc-20353999.

McHugh, Adam S. 2015. *The Listening LIfe: Embracing Attentiveness in a World of Distraction.* Downers Grove: InterVarsity Press.

Miller, Marlin E. 1990. "The church in the world as the community of the kingdom: a Radical Reformation perspective." *Brethren Life and Thought* 35 (1): 52-71. Accessed May 17, 2018. ATLA Religion Database with ATLASerials PLUS, EBSCOhost.

Moore, Michael S. 2003. *Faith Under Pressure: A Study of Biblical Leaders In Conflict*. Siloam Springs: Leafwood Publishers.

Osborn, George Thomas. 1933. "Why Did Decius and Valerian Proscribe Christianity?" *Church History 2* (2): 66-77. Accessed November 2018. http://www.jstor.org.fuller.idm.oclc.org/stable/3691999.

Plantinga, Richard J, Thomas R Thompson, and Matthew D Lundberg. 2010. *An Introduction to Christian Theology*. Cambridge: Cambridge University Press.

Pohlsander, Hans A. 1980. "Philip the Arab and Christianity." *Historia: Zaitschrift Fur Alte Geschichte* 29 (4): 463-73. Accessed November 2018. http://www.jstor.org.fuller.idm.oclc.org/stable/4435734.

Powell, Mark Allan. 2007. *What Do They Hear? Bridging The Gap Between Pulpit & Pew*. Nashville, Tennessee: Abingdon Press.

Rabbi Sacks, Jonathan. 2005. *To Heal A Fractured World: The Ethics of Responsibility*. New York: Schocken Bookk.

Rives, J. B. 1999. "The Decree of Decius and the Religion of Empire." *The Journal of Roman Studies* 89: 135-54. Accessed November 2018. doi:10.2307/300738.

Roberson, Loriann, and Carol T Kulik. 2007. "Stereotype Threat at Work." *Academy of Management Perspectives* (Academy of Management) 21 (2): 24-40. http://www.jstor.org.fuller.idm.oclc.org/stable/27747371.

Robinson, Mike. n.d. "Pastoral Care." *Barnabas Network International*. Accessed December 2018. http://www.barnabasnetwork.com/the_true_nature_of_pastoral_care.

Rosenbaum, PL, SD Walter, SE Hanna, and et al. 2002. "Prognosis for Gross Motor Function in Cerebral Palsy Creation of Motor Development Curves." *JAMA* 288.

Ryan, Roger. 2007. *Judges*. Sheffield, TN: Sheffield Phoenix Press.

Scheib, Karen D. 2016. *Pastoral Care: Telling the Stories of Our Lives.* Nashville: Abingdon Press.

Schwarz, Hans. 2000. *Eschatology.* Grand Rapids: William B. Eerdmans Publishing Company.

Seamands, Stephen. 2005. *Ministry in the Image of God: The Trinitarian Shape of Christian Service.* Downers Grove: InterVarsity Press.

Seamands, Stephen. 2005. "Relational Personhood: The Nature of Trinitarian Ministry." In *Ministry in the Image of God: The Trinitarian Shape of Christian Service,* by Stephen Seamands, 31-52. Downers Grove: InterVarsity Press.

Smail, Tom. 2005. *Like Father, Like Son: The Trinity Imagined in our Humanity.* Waynesboro, GA: Paternoster Press.

Steele, Claude M. 2010. *Whistling Vivaldi: How Stereotypes Affect Us and What We Can Do.* New York: W. W. Norton & Company.

Stets, Jan E, and Peter J Burke. 2000. "Identity Theory and Social Identity Theory." *Social Psychology Quarterly* (American Sociological Association) 63 (3): 224-237. http://www.jstor.org.fuller.idm.oclc.org/stable/2695870.

1996. "The Identity and Function of El/Baal Berith." *Journal of Biblical Literature* (The Society of Biblical Literature) 115 (3): 401-423. Accessed August 2018. doi:10.2307/3266894.

Voices, Critical. 2013. *How Racist Are You? - Jane Elliott's Blue Eyes/Brown Eyes Exercise.* February 11. https://youtu.be/Nqv9k3jbtYU.

Walters-Sleyon, George. 2013. "Studies on Religion and Recidivism: Focus on Roxbury, Dorchester, and Mattapan." *Trotter Review,* July 21: 21-45. http://scholarworks.umb.edu/trotter_review/vol21/iss1/4.

Watson, Donald L. 2014. *Diocletian.* February 02. Accessed 11 01, 2018. https://www.ancient.eu/Diocletian/.

Willard, Dallas. 1991. *The Spirit of Disciplines: Understanding How God Changes LIves*. Broadway: Harper Collins Publishers.

Willimon, William H. n.d. *The Theology and Practice of Ordained Ministry*. Nashville: Abingdon Press.

Workman, Herbert B. 1906. *Persecution in the Early Church*. Accessed 2018. https://search-ebscohost-com.fuller.idm.oclc.org/login.aspx?direct=true&db=h8h&AN=44521833&site=ehost-live.

Wray Beal, Lissa M. 2014. *Apollos Old Testament Commentary: 1 & 2 Kings*. Downers Grove: InterVarsity Press.

Yates, Kyle M. 1942. *Preaching From The Prophets*. 30th. Nashville, Tennessee: The Broadman Press.

Yee, Gale. 2007. *Judges & Methods New Approaches In Biblical Studies*. Minneapolis: Fortress Press.